A MAN FOR ALL SEASONS

Sir Thomas More
from the Holbein Portrait

More is a man of an angel's wit and singular learning; I know not his fellow. For where is the man of that gentleness, lowliness, and affability? And as time requireth a man of marvellous mirth and pastimes; and sometimes of as sad gravity: a man for all seasons.

Robert Whittinton

He was the person of the greatest virtue these islands ever produced.

Samuel Johnson

Robert Bolt

A MAN
FOR ALL SEASONS

A play of Sir Thomas More

Canadian Educational Edition

Notes and Questions by

E. R. Procunier, M.A.

Associate Professor of English
Althouse College of Education
The University of Western Ontario

BELLHAVEN HOUSE
AGINCOURT, CANADA

© Robert Bolt 1960

Notes, Questions, and Film Study © Bellhaven House

First published in this edition 1963
Second printing 1965
Revised edition (with film study) 1968
Second printing 1969
Third printing 1971
Fourth printing 1974

ISBN 0-88774-300-5

Published by
BELLHAVEN HOUSE LIMITED

Printed and bound in Canada by
THE BRYANT PRESS LIMITED

7 8 9 10 11 12 BP 82 81 80 79 78 77

CONTENTS

ROBERT BOLT

A Biographical Note

ROBERT BOLT was born in 1924 in Manchester, England, and attended the Grammar School and University in that city. Between 1943 and 1946 he was in the Royal Air Force and the British Army, and on his final discharge returned to Manchester University where he studied until 1949 and received a degree in History. After a year of post-graduate studies at Exeter University he became a school teacher, and from 1952 until 1958 taught English at Millfield School. Since 1958 he has devoted his time entirely to writing.

During his years as a teacher, Robert Bolt wrote a number of plays for radio which were broadcast by the B.B.C. He also did some producing, and has written one television play. His first stage play, *The Critic and the Heart*, was produced at the Oxford Playhouse in 1957, and in 1958 *Flowering Cherry* began a long run at the Haymarket Theatre in London with Sir Ralph Richardson and Celia Johnson. Two years later he had two more plays running in London, *A Man for All Seasons* at the Globe Theatre with Paul Scofield as Sir Thomas More, and *The Tiger and the Horse* at the Queen's Theatre with Sir Michael Redgrave, Catherine Lacey, and Vanessa Redgrave. *A Man for All Seasons* has been tremendously successful both in London and in New York. In 1962 the New York critics voted it the best foreign play of the year.

Robert Bolt's reputation as a dramatist rests on his ability to analyse emotion and the opposition of ideas. He is able to create a very strong impression with an imaginative use of gesture and the barest minimum of dialogue. It was because of these qualities in his work that he was chosen to write the script for the film *Lawrence of Arabia* which won the Best Picture Award in the 1962 Oscar Presentations. This was Mr. Bolt's first work for the screen, but he hopes to write further film scripts. His first allegiance, however, is to the theatre, and he has recently completed a play called *Gentle Jack*, written especially for England's most distinguished actress, Dame Edith Evans.

PREFACE

The bit of English History which is the background to this play is pretty well known. Henry VIII, who started with everything and squandered it all, who had the physical and mental fortitude to endure a lifetime of gratified greeds, the monstrous baby whom none dared gainsay, is one of the most popular figures in the whole procession. We recognise in him an archetype, one of the champions of our baser nature, and are in him vicariously indulged.

Against him stood the whole edifice of medieval religion, founded on piety, but by then as moneyed, elaborate, heaped high and inflexible as those abbey churches which Henry brought down with such a satisfying and disgraceful crash.

The collision came about like this: While yet a Prince, Henry did not expect to become a King for he had an elder brother, Arthur. A marriage was made between this Arthur and a Spanish Princess, Catherine, but Arthur presently died. The Royal Houses of Spain and England wished to repair the connection, and the obvious way to do it was to marry the young widow to Henry, now heir in Arthur's place. But Spain and England were Christian Monarchies and Christian law forbade a man to marry his brother's widow.

To be a Christian was to be a Churchman and there was only one Church (though plagued with many heresies) and the Pope was its head. At the request of Christian Spain and Christian England the Pope dispensed with the Christian law forbidding a man to marry his brother's widow, and when in due course Prince Henry ascended the English throne as Henry VIII, Catherine was his Queen.

For some years the marriage was successful; they respected and liked one another, and Henry took his pleasures elsewhere but lightly. However, at length he wished to divorce her.

The motives for such a wish are presumably as confused, inaccessible and helpless in a King as any other man, but here are three which make sense: Catherine had grown increasingly plain and intensely religious; Henry had fallen in love with Anne Boleyn; the Spanish alliance had become unpopular. None of these absolutely necessitated a divorce but there was a fourth that did. Catherine had not been able to provide Henry with a male child and was now presumed barren. There was a daughter, but competent statesmen were unanimous that a Queen on the throne of England was unthinkable. Anne and Henry were confident that between them they could produce a son; but if that son was to be Henry's heir, Anne would have to be Henry's wife.

The Pope was once again approached, this time by England only, and asked to declare the marriage with Catherine null, on the grounds that it contravened the Christian law which forbade marriage with a brother's widow. But England's insistence that the marriage had been null was now balanced by Spain's insistence that it hadn't. And at that moment Spain was well placed to influence the Pope's deliberations; Rome, where the Pope lived, had been very thoroughly sacked and occupied by Spanish troops. In addition one imagines a natural disinclination on the part of the Pope to have his powers turned on and off like a tap. At all events, after much ceremonious prevarication, while Henry waited with a rising temper, it became clear that so far as the Pope was concerned, the marriage with Catherine would stand.

To the ferment of a lover and the anxieties of a sovereign Henry now added a bad conscience; and a serious matter it was, for him and those about him.

The Bible, he found, was perfectly clear on such marriages as he had made with Catherine; they were forbidden. And the threatened penalty was exactly what had befallen him, the failure of male heirs. He was in a state of sin. He had been thrust into a state of sin by his father with the active help of the Pope. And the Pope now proposed to keep him in a state of sin. The man who would do that, it began to seem to Henry, had small claim to being the Vicar of God.

And indeed, on looking into the thing really closely, Henry found – what various voices had urged for centuries off and on – that the supposed Pope was no more than an ordinary Bishop, the Bishop of Rome. This made everything clear and everything possible. If the Pope was not a Pope at all but merely a bishop among bishops, then his special powers as Pope did not exist. In particular of course he had no power to dispense with God's rulings as revealed in Leviticus 18, but equally important, he had no power to appoint other Bishops; and here an ancient quarrel stirred.

For if the Pope had not the power to appoint bishops, then who did have, if not the King himself – King by the Grace of God? Henry's ancestors, all those other Henries, had been absolutely right; the Bishops of Rome, without a shadow of legality, had succeeded over the centuries in setting up a rival reign within the reign, a sort of long drawn usurpation. The very idea of it used to throw him into terrible rages. It should go on no longer.

He looked about for a good bishop to appoint to Canterbury, a bishop with no ambitions to modify God's ruling on deceased brothers' wives, yet sufficiently spirited to grant a divorce to his sovereign without consulting the Bishop of Rome. The man was to hand in Thomas Cranmer; Catherine was divorced, Anne married, and the Established Church of England was off on its singular way.

That, very roughly indeed, is the political, or theological, or politico-theological background to the play. But what of the social, or economic, or socio-economic, which we now think more important?

The economy was very progressive, the religion was very reactionary. We say therefore that the collision was inevitable, setting Henry aside as a colourful accident. With Henry presumably we set aside as accidents Catherine and Wolsey and Anne and More and Cranmer and Cromwell and the Lord Mayor of London and the man who cleaned his windows; setting indeed everyone aside as an accident, we say that the collision was inevitable. But that, on reflection, seems only to repeat that it happened. What is of interest is the way it happened, the way it was lived. For lived such collisions are. 'Religion' and 'economy' are abstractions which describe the way men live. Because men work we may speak of an economy, not the other way round. Because men worship we may speak of a religion, not the other way round. And when an economy collides with a religion it is living men who collide, nothing else (they collide with one another and within themselves).

Perhaps few people would disagree with that, put like that, and in theory. But in practice our theoreticians seem more and more to work the other way round, to derive the worker *from* his economy, the thinker *from* his culture, and we to derive even ourselves from our society and our location in it. When we ask ourselves 'What am I?' we may answer 'I am a Man' but are conscious that it's a silly answer because we don't know what kind of thing that might be; and feeling the answer silly we feel it's probably a silly question. We can't help asking it, however, for natural curiosity makes us ask it all the time of everyone else, and it would seem artificial to make ourselves the sole exception, would indeed envelop the mental image of our self in a unique silence and thus raise the question in a particularly disturbing way. So we answer of ourselves as we should of any other: 'This man here is a qualified surveyor, employed but with a view to partnership; this car he is driving has six cylinders and is almost new; he's doing all right; his opinions . . . ' and so on, describing ourselves to ourselves in terms more appropriate to somebody seen through a window. We think of ourselves in the Third Person.

To put it another way, more briefly; we no longer have, as past societies have had, any picture of individual Man (Stoic Philosopher, Christian Religious, Rational Gentleman) by which to recognise ourselves and against which to measure ourselves; we are anything. But if anything, then nothing, and it is not everyone who can live with that, though it is our true present position. Hence our willingness to locate ourselves from something that is certainly larger than ourselves, the society that contains us.

But society can only have as much idea as we have what we are about, for it has only our brains to think with. And the individual who tries to plot his position by reference to our society finds no fixed points, but only the vaunted absence of them, 'freedom' and 'opportunity'; freedom for what, opportunity to do what, is nowhere indicated. The only positive he is given is 'get and spend' ('get and spend – if you can' from the Right, 'get and spend – you deserve it' from the Left) and he did not need society to tell him that. In other words we are thrown back by our society upon ourselves at our lowest, that is at our least satisfactory to ourselves. Which of course sends us flying back to society with all the force of rebound.

Socially, we fly from the idea of an individual to the professional describers, the classifiers, the men with the categories and a quick ear for the latest sub-division, who flourish among us like priests. Individually, we do what we can to describe and classify ourselves and so assure ourselves that from the outside at least we do have a definite outline. Both socially and individually it is with us as it is with our cities – an accelerating flight to the periphery, leaving a centre which is empty when the hours of business are over.

That is an ambitious style of thinking, and pride cometh before a fall, but it was with some such ideas in mind that I started on this play. Or else they developed as I wrote it. Or else I have developed them in defence of it now that it is written. It is not easy to know what a play is 'about' until it is finished, and by then what it is 'about' is incorporated in it irreversibly and is no more to be separated from it than the shape of a statue is to be separated from the marble. Writing a play is thinking, not thinking about thinking; more like a dream than a scheme – except that it lasts six months or more, and that one is responsible for it.

At any rate, Thomas More, as I wrote about him, became for me a man with an adamantine sense of his own self. He knew where he began and left off, what area of himself he could yield to the encroachments of his enemies, and what to the encroachments of those he loved. It was a substantial area in both cases for he had a proper sense of fear and was a busy lover. Since he was a clever man and a great lawyer he was able to retire from those areas in wonderfully good order, but at length he was asked to retreat from that final area where he located his self. And there this supple, humorous, unassuming and sophisticated person set like metal, was overtaken by an absolutely primitive rigour, and could no more be budged than a cliff.

This account of him developed as I wrote: what first attracted me was a person who could not be accused of any incapacity for life, who indeed seized life in great variety and almost greedy quantities, who nevertheless found something in himself without which life was valueless and when that was denied him was able to grasp his death. For there can be no doubt, given the circumstances, that he did it himself. If, on any day up to that of his execution, he had been willing to give public approval to Henry's marriage with Anne Boleyn, he could have gone on living. Of course the marriage was associated with other things – the attack on the abbeys, the whole Reformation policy – to which More was violently opposed, but I think he could have found his way round that; he showed every sign of doing so. Unfortunately his approval of the marriage was asked for in a form that required him to state that he believed what he didn't believe, and required him to state it on oath.

This brings me to something for which I feel the need to explain, perhaps apologise. More was a very orthodox Catholic and for him an oath was something perfectly specific; it was an invitation to God, an invitation God would not refuse, to act as a witness, and to judge; the consequence of perjury was damnation, for More another perfectly specific concept. So for More the issue was simple (though remembering the outcome it can hardly have been easy). But I am not a Catholic nor even in the meaningful sense of the word a Christian. So by what right do I appropriate a Christian Saint to my purposes? Or to put it the other way, why do I take as my hero a man who brings about his own death because he can't put his hand on an old black book and tell an ordinary lie?

For this reason: A man takes an oath only when he wants to commit himself quite exceptionally to the statement, when he wants to make an identity between the truth of it and his own virtue; he offers himself as a guarantee. And it works. There is a special kind of shrug for a perjurer; we feel that the man has no self to commit, no guarantee to offer. Of course it's much less effective now that for most of us the actual words of the oath are not much more than impressive mumbo-jumbo than it was when they made obvious sense; we would prefer most men to guarantee their statements with, say, cash rather than with themselves. We feel – we know – the self to be an equivocal commodity. There are fewer and fewer things which, as they say, we 'cannot bring ourselves' to do. We can find almost no limits for ourselves other than the physical, which being physical are not optional. Perhaps this is why we have fallen back so widely on physical torture as a means of bringing pressure to bear on one another. But though few of us have anything in ourselves like an immortal soul which we regard as absolutely inviolable, yet most of us still feel some-

thing which we should prefer, on the whole, not to violate.
Most men feel when they swear an oath (the marriage vow for
example) that they have invested something. And from this it's
possible to guess what an oath must be to a man for whom it is
not merely a time-honoured and understood ritual but also a
definite contract. It may be that a clear sense of the self can
only crystallize round something transcendental in which case,
our prospects look poor, for we are rightly committed to the
rational. I think the paramount gift our thinkers, artists, and
for all I know, our men of science, should labour to get for us
is a sense of selfhood without resort to magic. Albert Camus is
a writer I admire in this connection.

Anyway, the above must serve as my explanation and
apology for treating Thomas More, a Christian Saint, as a hero
of selfhood.

Another thing that attracted me to this amazing man was his
splendid social adjustment. So far from being one of society's
sore teeth he was, like the hero of Camus' *La Chute*, almost
indecently successful. He was respectably not nobly born, in
the merchant class, the progressive class of the epoch, distinguished himself first as a scholar, then as a lawyer, was made
an Ambassador, finally Lord Chancellor. A visitors' book at
his house in Chelsea would have looked like a Sixteenth Century *Who's Who*: Holbein, Erasmus, Colet, everybody. He cor-
responded with the greatest minds in Europe as the repre-
sentative and acknowledged champion of the New Learning in
England. He was a friend of the King, who would send for
More when his social appetites took a turn in that direction and
once walked round the Chelsea garden with his arm round
More's neck. ('If my head would win him a castle in France, it
should not fail to fall', said More.) He adored and was adored
by his own large family. He parted with more than most men
when he parted with his life, for he accepted and enjoyed his
social context.

One sees that there is no necessary contradiction here; it is

society after all which proffers an oath and with it the opportunity for perjury. But why did a man so utterly absorbed
in his society, at one particular point disastrously part company
from it? How indeed was it possible – unless there was some
sudden aberration? But that explanation won't do, because
he continued to the end to make familiar and confident use of
society's weapons, tact, favour, and above all, the letter of the
law.

For More again the answer to this question would be perfectly
simple (though again not easy); the English Kingdom, his
immediate society, was subservient to the larger society of the
Church of Christ, founded by Christ, extending over Past and
Future, ruled from Heaven. There are still some for whom
that is perfectly simple, but for most it can only be a metaphor.
I took it as a metaphor for that larger context which we all
inhabit, the terrifying cosmos. Terrifying because no laws, no
sanctions, no *mores* obtain there; it is either empty or occupied
by God and Devil nakedly at war. The sensible man will seek to
live his life without dealings with this larger environment,
treating it as as a fine spectacle on a clear night, or a subject for
innocent curiosity. At the most he will allow himself an agree-
able *frisson* when he contemplates his own relation to the cosmos, but he will not try to live in it; he will gratefully accept the
shelter of his society. This was certainly More's intention.

If 'society' is the name we give to human behaviour when it
is patterned and orderly, then the Law (extending from empir-
ical traffic regulations, through the mutating laws of property,
and on to the great tabus like incest and patricide) is the very
pattern of society. More's trust in the law was his trust in his
society; his desperate sheltering beneath the forms of the law
was his determination to remain within the shelter of society.
Cromwell's contemptuous shattering of the forms of law by
an unconcealed act of perjury showed how fragile for any individual is that shelter. Legal or illegal had no further meaning,
the social references had been removed. More was offered to be

sure, the chance of slipping back into the society which had thrust him out into the warring cosmos, but even in that solitude he found himself able to repeat, or continue, the decision he had made while he still enjoyed the common shelter.

I see that I have used a lot of metaphors. I know no other way to treat this subject. In the play I used for this theme a poetic image. As a figure for the superhuman context I took the largest, most alien, least formulated thing I know, the sea and water. The references to ships, rivers, currents, tides, navigation, and so on, are all used for this purpose. Society by contrast figures as dry land. I set out with no very well formed idea of the kind of play it was to be, except that it was not to be naturalistic. The possibility of using imagery, that is of using metaphors not decoratively but with an intention, was a side effect of that. It's a very far from new idea, of course. Whether it worked I rather doubt. Certainly no-one noticed. But I comfort myself with the thought that it's the nature of imagery to work, in performance at any rate, unconsciously. But if, as I think, a play is more like a poem than a straight narration, still less a demonstration or lecture, then imagery ought to be important. It's perhaps necessary to add that by a poem I mean something tough and precise, not something dreamy. As Brecht said, beauty and form of language are a primary alienation device. I was guaranteed some beauty and form by incorporating passages from Sir Thomas More himself. For the rest my concern was to match with these as best I could so that the theft should not be too obvious.

In two previous plays, *Flowering Cherry* and *The Tiger and the Horse*, I had tried, but with fatal timidity, to handle contemporaries in a style that should make them larger than life; in the first mainly by music and mechanical effects, in the second mainly by making the characters unnaturally articulate and unnaturally aware of what they 'stood for'. Inevitably these plays looked like what they most resembled, orthodox fourth wall dramas with puzzling, uncomfortable, and, if you are un-charitable, pretentious overtones. So for this one I took a historical setting in the hope that the distance of years would give me Dutch courage, and enable me to treat my characters in a properly heroic, properly theatrical manner.

The style I eventually used was a bastardized version of the one most recently associated with Bertolt Brecht. This is not the place to discuss that style at any length, but it does seem to me that the style practised by Brecht differs from the style taught by Brecht, or taught to us by his disciples. Perhaps they are more Royalist than the King. Or perhaps there was something daimonic in Brecht the artist which could not submit to Brecht the teacher. That would explain why in the *Chalk Circle*, which is to demonstrate that goodness is a terrible temptation, goodness triumphs very pleasantly. And why in *Mother Courage*, which is to demonstrate the unheroic nature of war, the climax is an act of heroism which Rider Haggard might have balked at. And why in *Galileo*, which is to demonstrate the social and objective value of scientific knowledge, Galileo, congratulated on saving his skin so as to augment that knowledge, is made to deny its value on the grounds that he defaulted at the moment when what the world needed was for one man to be true to himself. I am inclined to think that it is simply that Brecht was a very fine artist, and that life is complicated and ambivalent. At all events I agree with Eric Bentley that the proper effect of alienation is to enable the audience *reculer pour mieux sauter*, to deepen, not to terminate, their involvement in the play.

Simply to slap your audience in the face satisfies an austere and puritanical streak which runs in many of his disciples and sometimes, detrimentally I think, in Brecht himself. But it is a dangerous game to play. It has the effect of shock because it is unexpected. But it is unexpected only because it flies in the face of a thoroughly established convention. (A convention which goes far beyond naturalism; briefly, the convention that the actors are there as actors, not as themselves.) Each time it is done

B

it is a little less unexpected, so that a bigger and bigger dosage will be needed to produce the same effect. If it were continued indefinitely it would finally not be unexpected at all. The theatrical convention would then have been entirely dissipated and we should have in the theatre a situation with one person, who used to be an actor, desperately trying to engage the attention – by rude gestures, loud noises, indecent exposure, fireworks, anything – of other persons, who used to be the audience. As this point was approached some very lively evenings might be expected, but the depth and subtlety of the notions which can be communicated by such methods may be doubted. When we use alienation methods just for kicks, we in the theatre are sawing through the branch on which we are sitting.

I tried then for a 'bold and beautiful verbal architecture', a story rather than a plot, and overtly theatrical means of switching from one locale to another. I also used the most notorious of the alienation devices, an actor who addresses the audience and comments on the action. But I had him address the audience in character, that is from within the play.

He is intended to draw the audience into the play, not thrust them off it. In this respect he largely fails, and for a reason I had not foreseen. He is called 'The Common Man' (just as there is a character called 'The King') and the word 'common' was intended primarily to indicate 'that which is common to us all'. But he was taken instead as a portrayal of that mythical beast The Man In The Street. This in itself was not so bad; after all he was intended to be something with which everyone would be able to identify. But once he was identified as common in that sense, my character was by one party accepted as a properly belittling account of that vulgar person, and by another party bitterly resented on his behalf. (Myself I had meant him to be attractive, and his philosophy impregnable.) What both these parties had in common – if I may use the word – is that they thought of him as somebody else. Wherever he might have been, this Common Man, he was certainly not in the theatre. He is harder to find than a unicorn. But I must modify that. He was not in the Stalls, among his fashionable detractors and defenders. But in the laughter this character drew down from the Gallery, that laughter which is the most heartening sound our Theatre knows, I thought I heard once or twice a rueful note of recognition.

September 1960

PEOPLE IN THE PLAY

THE COMMON MAN: Late middle age. He wears from head to foot black tights which delineate his pot-bellied figure. His face is crafty, loosely benevolent, its best expression that of base humour.

SIR THOMAS MORE: Late forties. Pale, middle-sized, not robust. But the life of the mind in him is so abundant and debonair that it illuminates the body. His movements are open and swift but never wild, having a natural moderation. The face is intellectual and quickly delighted, the norm to which it returns serious and compassionate. Only in moments of high crisis does it become ascetic — though then freezingly.

RICHARD RICH: Early thirties. A good body unexercised. A studious unhappy face lit by the fire of banked down appetite. He is an academic, hounded by self-doubt to enter the world of affairs, and longing to be rescued from himself.

DUKE OF NORFOLK: Late forties. Heavy, active, a sportsman and soldier held together by rigid adherence to the minimal code of conventional duty. Attractively aware of his moral and intellectual insignificance, but also a great nobleman, untouchably convinced that his acts and ideas are important because they are his.

ALICE MORE: Late forties. Born into the merchant class, now a great lady, she is absurd at a distance, impressive close to. Overdressed, coarsely fashioned, she worships society; brave, hot-hearted, she worships her husband. In consequence, troubled by and defiant towards both.

MARGARET MORE: Middle twenties. A beautiful girl of ardent moral fineness; she both suffers and shelters behind a reserved stillness which it is her father's care to mitigate.

CARDINAL WOLSEY: Old. A big decayed body in scarlet. An almost megalomaniac ambition unhappily matched by an excelling intellect, he now inhabits a lonely den of self-indulgence and contempt.

THOMAS CROMWELL: Late thirties. Subtle and serious; the face expressing not inner tension but the tremendous outgoing will of the renaissance. A self-conceit that can cradle gross crimes in the name of effective action. In short an intellectual bully.

CHAPUYS: Sixties. A professional diplomat and lay ecclesiastic dressed in black. Much on his dignity as a man of the world he in fact trots happily along a mental footpath as narrow as a peasant's.

CHAPUYS' ATTENDANT: An apprentice diplomat of good family.

WILLIAM ROPER: Early thirties; a stiff body and an immobile face. Little imagination, moderate brain, but an all consuming rectitude which is his cross, his solace, and his hobby.

THE KING: *Not* the Holbein Henry, but a much younger man, clean-shaven, bright-eyed, graceful and athletic. The Golden Hope of the New Learning throughout Europe. Only the levity with which he handles his absolute power foreshadows his future corruption.

A WOMAN: Middle fifties. Self-opinionated, self-righteous, selfish, indignant.

CRANMER: Late forties. Sharp-minded, sharp-faced. He treats the Church as a job of administration and theology as a set of devices, for he lacks personal religiosity.

———— ◦‣◦◦‣◦ ————

THE SET is the same throughout but capable of varied lightings, as indicated. Its form is finally a matter for the designer, but to some extent is dictated by the action of the play. I have visualised two galleries of flattened Tudor arches, one above the other, able to be entered from off-stage. A flight of stairs leading from the upper gallery to the stage. A projection which can suggest an alcove or closet, with a tapestry curtain to be drawn across it. A table and some chairs, sufficiently heavy to be congruous indoors or out.

THE COSTUMES are also a matter for the designer, but I have visualised no exact reproductions of the elaborate style of the period. I think plain colours should be used, thus scarlet for the Cardinal, grey for More, gold for the King, green for the Duke, blue for Margaret, black and pinstripe for the administrators Rich and Cromwell, and so on.

A Man For All Seasons *was first presented by H. M. Tennent Limited at the Globe Theatre in London, England, on July 1st, 1960, with the following cast:*

The Common Man	Leo McKern
Thomas More	Paul Scofield
Richard Rich	John Brown
The Duke of Norfolk	Alexander Gauge
Alice More	Wynne Clark
Margaret More	Pat Keen
Cardinal Wolsey	Willoughby Goddard
Thomas Cromwell	Andrew Keir
The Spanish Ambassador	Geoffrey Dunn
The Ambassador's Attendant	Brian Harrison
William Roper	John Carson
King Henry VIII	Richard Leech
The Woman	Beryl Andrews
Cranmer, Archbishop of Canterbury	William Roderick

Directed by Noël Willman. *Settings, Costumes by* Motley.

The first presentation in North America was by Robert Whitehead and Roger L. Stevens at the ANTA Theatre, New York City, on November 22nd, 1961, with the following cast:

The Common Man	George Rose
Sir Thomas More	Paul Scofield
Richard Rich	William Redfield
The Duke of Norfolk	Albert Dekker
Alice More	Carol Goodner
Margaret More	Olga Bellin
Cardinal Wolsey	Jack Creley
Thomas Cromwell	Leo McKern
The Spanish Ambassador	David J. Stewart
The Ambassador's Attendant	John Colenback
William Roper	Peter Brandon
King Henry VIII	Keith Baxter
The Woman	Sarah Burton
Cranmer, Archbishop of Canterbury	Lester Rawlins

Directed by Noël Willman. *Settings, Costumes by* Motley. *Lighting by* Paul Morrison. *Produced by arrangement with* H. M. Tennent Limited.

ACT ONE

When the curtain rises, the set is in darkness but for a single spot which descends vertically upon the COMMON MAN, *who stands in front of a big property basket.*

COMMON MAN: It is perverse! To start a play made up of Kings and Cardinals in speaking costumes and intellectuals with embroidered mouths, with me.

If a King, or a Cardinal had done the prologue he'd have had the right materials. And an intellectual would have shown enough majestic meanings, coloured propositions, and closely woven liturgical stuff to dress the House of Lords! But this!

Is this a costume? Does this say anything? It barely covers one man's nakedness! A bit of black material to reduce Old Adam to the Common Man.

Oh, if they'd let me come on naked, I could have shown you something of my own. Which would have told you without words——! . . . Something I've forgotten . . . Old Adam's muffled up.

(*Backing towards basket.*) Well, for a proposition of my own, I need a costume. (*Takes out and puts on the coat and hat of* STEWARD.)

Matthew! The Household Steward of Sir Thomas More! (*Lights come up swiftly on set. He takes from the basket five silver goblets, one larger than the others, and a jug with a lid, with which he furnishes the table. A burst of conversational merriment off; he pauses and indicates head of stairs.*) There's company to dinner. (*Finishes business at table.*)

1

All right! A Common Man! A Sixteenth-Century Butler!
(*He drinks from the jug.*) All right – the Six—— (*Breaks off,
agreeably surprised by the quality of the liquor, regards the jug
respectfully and drinks again.*) The Sixteenth Century is the
Century of the Common Man. (*Puts down the jug.*) Like all
the other centuries. (*Crossing right.*) And that's my proposition.

    *During the last part of the speech, voices off. Now, enter, at head
of stairs,* SIR THOMAS MORE.

STEWARD: That's Sir Thomas More.

MORE: The wine please, Matthew?

STEWARD: It's there, Sir Thomas.

MORE (*looking into jug*): Is it good?

STEWARD: Bless you, sir! *I* don't know.

MORE (*mildly*): Bless you too, Matthew.

    Enter RICH *at head of stairs.*

RICH (*enthusiastically pursuing an argument*): But every man has
his price!

STEWARD (*contemptuous*): Master Richard Rich.

RICH: But yes! In money too.

MORE (*gentle impatience*): No no no.

RICH: Or pleasure. Titles, women, bricks-and-mortar, there's
always something.

MORE: Childish.

RICH: Well, in suffering, certainly.

MORE (*interested*): Buy a man with suffering?

RICH: Impose suffering, and offer him – escape.

MORE: Oh. For a moment I thought you were being profound.
(*Gives cup to* RICH.)

RICH (*to* STEWARD): Good evening, Matthew.

STEWARD (*snubbing*): 'Evening, sir.

RICH: No, not a bit profound; it then becomes a purely
practical question of how to make him suffer sufficiently.

MORE: Mm. . . . (*Takes him by the arm and walks with him.*) And
. . . who recommended you to read Signor Machiavelli?

(RICH *breaks away laughing; a fraction too long.* MORE *smiles.*)
No, who? (*More laughter.*) . . . Mm?

RICH: Master Cromwell.

MORE: Oh. . . . (*Back to the wine jug and cups.*) He's a very able man.

RICH: And so he is!

MORE: Yes, I say he is. He's very able.

RICH: And he will do something for me, he says.

MORE: I didn't know you knew him.

RICH: Pardon me, Sir Thomas, but how much do you know about me?

MORE: Whatever you've let me know.

RICH: I've let you know everything!

MORE: Richard, you should go back to Cambridge; you're deteriorating.

RICH: Well, I'm not used! . . . D'you know how much I have to show for seven months' work——

MORE: – Work?

RICH: – Work! Waiting's work when you wait as I wait, hard! . . . For seven months, that's two hundred days, I have to show: the acquaintance of the Cardinal's outer doorman, the indifference of the Cardinal's inner doorman, and the Cardinal's chamberlain's hand in my chest! . . . Oh – also one half of a Good Morning delivered at fifty paces by the Duke of Norfolk. Doubtless he mistook me for someone.

MORE: He was very affable at dinner.

RICH: Oh, everyone's affable *here*. . . . (MORE *is pleased.*) Also of course, the friendship of Sir Thomas More. Or should I say acquaintance?

MORE: Say friendship.

RICH: Well, there! 'A friend of Sir Thomas and still no office? There must be something wrong with him.'

MORE: I thought we said friendship. . . . (*Considers; then.*) The Dean of St Paul's offers you a post; with a house, a servant and fifty pounds a year.

RICH: What? What post?

MORE: At the new school.

RICH (*bitterly disappointed*): A teacher!

MORE: A man should go where he won't be tempted. Look, Richard, see this. (*Hands a silver cup.*) Look. . . . Look. . . .

RICH: Beautiful.

MORE: Italian. . . . Do you want it?

RICH: Why——?

MORE: No joke; keep it; or sell it.

RICH: Well I—— Thank you of course—— Thank you! Thank you! But——?

MORE: You'll sell it, won't you?

RICH: Yes, I think so. Yes, I will.

MORE: And buy, what?

RICH (*sudden ferocity*): Some decent clothes!

MORE (*with sympathy*): Ah.

RICH: I want a gown like yours.

MORE: You'll get several gowns for that I should think. It was sent to me a little while ago by some woman. Now she's put a lawsuit into the Court of Requests. It's a bribe, Richard.

RICH: Oh. . . . (*Chagrined.*) So you give it away of course.

MORE: Yes!

RICH: To me?

MORE: Well, I'm not going to keep it, and you need it. Of course – if you feel it's contaminated . . .

RICH: No, no. I'll risk it. (*Both smile.*)

MORE: But, Richard, in office they offer you all sorts of things. I was once offered a whole village, with a mill, and a manor house, and heaven knows what else – a coat of arms I shouldn't be surprised. Why not be a teacher? You'd be a fine teacher. Perhaps, a great one.

RICH: And if I was who would know it?

MORE: You, your pupils, your friends, God. Not a bad public, that. . . . Oh, and a *quiet* life.

RICH (*laughing*): *You* say that!

MORE: Richard, I was commanded into office; it was inflicted on me. . . . (RICH *regards him.*) Can't you believe that?

RICH: It's hard.

MORE (*grimly*): Be a teacher.

Enter at head of stairs NORFOLK.

STEWARD (*to audience*): The Duke of Norfolk. A lord.

NORFOLK: I tell you he stooped from the clouds! (*Breaks off, irritable.*) Alice!

Enter instantly at head of stairs ALICE.

ALICE (*irritable*): Here!

STEWARD (*to audience*): Lady Alice. My master's wife.

NORFOLK: I tell you he stooped——

ALICE: – He didn't——

NORFOLK: – Goddammit he did——

ALICE: – Couldn't——

NORFOLK: – He *does*——

ALICE: – Not possible——

NORFOLK: – But *often*——

ALICE: Never.

NORFOLK: Well, damn my soul! (*Takes wine.*) Thank you, Thomas.

MORE (*to* MARGARET, *having appeared on gallery*): Come down, Meg.

STEWARD (*to audience, soapy*): Lady Margaret, my master's daughter, lovely; really lovely.

ALICE (*glances suspiciously at* STEWARD): Matthew, get about your business. (*Exit* STEWARD.) We'll settle this, my lord, we'll put it to Thomas. Thomas, no falcon could stoop from a cloud, could it?

MORE: I don't know, my dear; it sounds unlikely. I have seen falcons do some very splendid things.

ALICE: But how could he stoop from a cloud? He couldn't see where he was going.

NORFOLK: You see, Alice – you're ignorant of the subject; a real falcon don't *care* where he's going! Anyway, I'm talking to Meg. (*A sportsman's story.*) 'Twas the very first cast of the day, Meg; the sun was behind us. And from side to side of the valley like the roof of a tent, was solid mist——

ALICE: Oh, mist.

NORFOLK: Well, mist is cloud isn't it?

ALICE: No.

RICH: The opinion of Aristotle is that mists are an exhalation of the earth whereas clouds——

NORFOLK: He stooped five hundred feet! Like *that*! Like an Act of God isn't he, Thomas?

MORE: He's tremendous.

NORFOLK (*to* ALICE): Tremendous.

MARGARET: Did he kill the heron?

NORFOLK: Oh, the *heron* was *clever*. (*Very discreditable evidently.*) It was a royal stoop though. (*Sly.*) If you could ride, Alice, I'd show you.

ALICE (*hotly*): I can ride, my lord!

MORE: No, no, you'll make yourself ill.

ALICE: And I'll bet – twenty-five – no thirty shillings I see no falcon stoop from no cloud!

NORFOLK: Done.

MORE: Alice – you can't ride with *them*.

ALICE: God's body, Thomas, remember who you are. Am I a City Wife?

MORE: No indeed, you've just lost thirty shillings I think; there *are* such birds. And the heron got home to his chicks, Meg, so everything was satisfactory.

MARGARET (*smiling*): Yes.

MORE: What was that of Aristotle's, Richard?

RICHARD: Nothing, Sir Thomas – 'twas out of place.

NORFOLK (*to* RICH): I've never found much use in Aristotle myself, not practically. Great philosopher of course. Wonderful mind.

RICH: Exactly, Your Grace!

NORFOLK (*suspicious*): Eh?

MORE: Master Rich is newly converted to the doctrines of Machiavelli.

RICH: Oh *no*...!

NORFOLK: Oh, the Italian. Nasty book, from what I hear.

MARGARET: Very practical, Your Grace.

NORFOLK: You read it? Amazing girl, Thomas, but where are you going to find a husband for her?

MORE (MORE *and* MEG *exchange a glance*): Where indeed?

RICH: The doctrines of Machiavelli have been largely mistaken I think; indeed properly apprehended he has no doctrine. Master Cromwell has the sense of it I think when he says——

NORFOLK: You know Cromwell?

RICH: ... Slightly, Your Grace...

NORFOLK: The Cardinal's Secretary. (*Exclamations of shock from* MORE, MARGARET *and* ALICE.) It's a fact.

MORE: When, Howard?

NORFOLK: Two, three days.

They move about uneasily.

ALICE: A *farrier's* son?

NORFOLK: Well, the Cardinal's a butcher's son, isn't he?

ALICE: It'll be up quick and down quick with Master Cromwell.

NORFOLK *grunts.*

MORE (*quietly*): Did you know this?

RICH: No!

MARGARET: Do you *like* Master Cromwell, Master Rich?

ALICE: He's the only man in London if he does!

RICH: I think I do, Lady Alice!

MORE (*pleased*): Good. ... Well, you don't need *my* help now.

RICH: Sir Thomas, if only you knew how much, much rather I'd yours than his!

Enter STEWARD *at head of stairs. Descends and gives letter to* MORE *who opens it and reads.*

MORE: Talk of the Cardinal's Secretary and the Cardinal appears. He wants me. Now.

ALICE: At this time of the night?

MORE (*mildly*): The King's business.

ALICE: The Queen's business.

NORFOLK: More than likely, Alice, more than likely.

MORE (*cuts in sharply*): What's the time?

STEWARD: Eleven o'clock, sir.

MORE: Is there a boat?

STEWARD: Waiting, sir.

MORE (*to* ALICE *and* MARGARET): Go to bed. You'll excuse me, Your Grace? Richard? (*Kisses wife and daughter.*) Now you'll go to bed. . . . (*The* MORE *family, as a matter of routine, put their hands together and:*)

MORE ⎱ Dear Lord give us rest tonight, or if we must
ALICE ⎰ be wakeful, cheerful. Careful only for our
MARGARET ⎰ soul's salvation. For Christ's sake. Amen.

MORE: And Bless our Lord the King.

ALICE ⎱ And Bless our Lord the King.
MARGARET ⎰

ALL: Amen.

And then immediately a brisk leave-taking, MORE *moving off below, the others mounting the stairs.*

MORE: Howard, are *you* at Richmond?

NORFOLK: No, down the river.

MORE: Then good night! (*Sees* RICH *disconsolate.*) Oh, Your Grace, here's a young man desperate for employment. Something in the clerical line.

NORFOLK: Well, if you recommend him.

MORE: No, I don't recommend him; but I point him out. (*Moving off.*) He's at the New Inn. You could take him there.

NORFOLK (*to* RICH *mounting stairs*): All right, come on.

RICH: My Lord.

NORFOLK: We'll hawk at Hounslow, Alice.

ALICE: Wherever you like. (ALICE *and* MARGARET *follow* NORFOLK.)

RICH (*at foot of stairs*): Sir Thomas! . . . (MORE *turns.*) Thank you.

MORE: Be a teacher. (*Moving off again.*) Oh—— The ground's hard at Hounslow, Alice!

NORFOLK: Eh? (*Delighted roar.*) That's where the Cardinal crushed his bum!

MORE ⎫
NORFOLK ⎬ Good night! Good night!
ALICE ⎪
RICH ⎭

They process off along the gallery.

MORE (*softly*): Margaret!

MARGARET: Yes?

MORE: Go to bed.

MARGARET *exits above,* MORE *exits below. After a moment* RICH *walks swiftly back down stage, picks up the goblet and is going off with it.*

STEWARD: Eh!

RICH: What——! Oh. . . . It's a gift, Matthew. Sir Thomas gave it to me. (STEWARD *takes it and regards it silently.*) He gave it to me.

STEWARD (*returns it*): Very nice present, sir.

RICH (*backing away with it*): Yes. Good night, Matthew.

STEWARD: Sir Thomas has taken quite a fancy to you, sir.

RICH: Er, here—— (*Gives money and goes.*)

STEWARD: Thank you sir. . . . (*To audience.*) That one'll come to nothing. (*Begins packing props into basket. Pauses with cup in hand.*) My master Thomas More would give anything to anyone. Some say that's good and some say that's bad, but I say he can't help it – and that's bad . . . because some day someone's going to ask him for something that he wants to keep; and he'll be out of practice. (*Puts cloth with papers, ink, etc., on table.*) There must be something that he wants to keep. That's only Common Sense.

Enter WOLSEY. *He sits at table and immediately commences writing, watched by* COMMON MAN *who then exits. Enter* MORE.

WOLSEY (*writing*): It's half-past one. Where've you been? (*Bell strikes one.*)

MORE: One o'clock, Your Grace. I've been on the river.

    WOLSEY *writes in silence, while* MORE *waits standing.*

WOLSEY (*still writing, pushes paper across table*): Since you seemed so violently opposed to the Latin dispatch, I thought you'd like to look it over.

MORE (*touched*): Thank you, Your Grace.

WOLSEY: Before it goes.

MORE (*smiles*): Your Grace is very kind. (*Takes and reads.*) Thank you.

WOLSEY: Well, what d'you think of it? (*He is still writing.*)

MORE: It seems very well phrased, Your Grace.

WOLSEY (*permits himself a chuckle*): The devil it does! (*Sits back.*)

And apart from the style, Sir Thomas?

MORE: I think the Council should be told before that goes to Italy.

WOLSEY: Would you tell the Council? Yes, I believe you would. You're a constant regret to me, Thomas. If you could just see facts flat on, without that moral squint; with just a little common sense, you could have been a statesman.

MORE (*little pause*): Oh, Your Grace flatters me.

WOLSEY: Don't frivel. . . . Thomas, are you going to help me?

MORE (*hesitates, looks away*): If Your Grace will be specific.

WOLSEY: Ach, you're a plodder! Take you altogether, Thomas, your scholarship, your experience, what are you? (*A single trumpet calls, distant, frosty and clear.* WOLSEY *gets up and goes and looks from window.*) Come here. (MORE *joins him.*) The King.

MORE: Yes.

WOLSEY: Where has he been? D'you know?

MORE: I, Your Grace?

WOLSEY: Oh, spare me your discretion. He's been to play in the muck again. *contemptuous*

MORE (*coldly*): Indeed.

WOLSEY: Indeed! Indeed! Are you going to oppose me? (*Trumpet again.* WOLSEY *visibly relaxes.*) He's gone in. . . . (*Leaves window.*) All right, we'll plod. The King wants a son; what are you going to do about it?

MORE (*dry murmur*): I'm very sure the King needs no advice from me on what to do about it.

WOLSEY (*from behind grips his shoulder fiercely*): Thomas, we're alone. *lie* I give you my word. There's no one here.

MORE: I didn't suppose there was, Your Grace. *state informer*

WOLSEY: Oh. (*Goes to table, sits, signs* MORE *to sit.* MORE *unsuspectingly obeys. Then, deliberately loud.*) Do you favour a change of dynasty, Sir Thomas? D'you think two Tudors is sufficient? *— attempts to provoke More into some treasonable indiscretion*

MORE (*starting up in horrified alarm*): – For God's sake, Your Grace——!

WOLSEY: Then the King needs a son; I repeat what are you going to do about it?

MORE (*steadily*): I pray for it daily.

WOLSEY (*snatches up candle and holds to* MORE'*s face. Softly*): God's death, he means it. . . . That thing out there's at least fertile, Thomas. *symbolic light, reasonableness, peace, it is extinguished*

MORE: But she's not his wife.

WOLSEY: No, Catherine's his wife and she's as barren as brick. Are you going to pray for a miracle? *more to More*

MORE: There *are* precedents.——

WOLSEY: Yes. All right. Good. Pray. Pray by all means. But in addition to Prayer there is Effort. My effort's to secure a divorce. Have I your support or have I not? *cynical dismissal – lack of religious feeling*

MORE (*sits*): A dispensation was given so that the King might marry Queen Catherine, for state reasons. Now we are to ask the Pope to – dispense with his dispensation, also for state reasons?

WOLSEY: – I don't *like* plodding, Thomas, don't make me plod longer than I have to—— Well?

MORE: Then clearly all we have to do is approach His Holiness and ask him.

The pace becomes rapid.

WOLSEY: – I think we might influence His Holiness' answer——

MORE :– Like this? – (*The dispatch.*)

WOLSEY: – Like that and in other ways——

MORE: – I've already expressed my opinion on this——

WOLSEY: – Then, good night! Oh, your conscience is your own affair; but you're a statesman! Do you *remember* the Yorkist Wars?

MORE: Very clearly.

WOLSEY: Let him die without an heir and we'll have them back again. Let him die without an heir and this 'peace' you think so much of will go out like that! (*Extinguishes candle.*) Very well, then England needs an heir; certain measures, perhaps regrettable, perhaps not – (*pompous*) there is much in the Church that *needs* reformation, Thomas—— (MORE *smiles.*) All right, regrettable! But necessary, to get us an heir! Now explain how you as Councillor of England can obstruct those measures for the sake of your own, private, conscience.

MORE: Well . . . I believe, when statesmen forsake their own private conscience for the sake of their public duties . . . they lead their country by a short route to chaos. (*During this speech he relights the candle with another.*) And we shall have my prayers to fall back on.

WOLSEY: You'd like that, wouldn't you? To govern the country by prayers?

MORE: Yes, I should.

WOLSEY: I'd like to be there when you try. Who *will* deal

Successor of Lord Chancellorship

with all this – paper, after me? You? Fisher? Suffolk?

MORE: Fisher for me.

WOLSEY: Aye, but for the King. What about my Secretary, Master Cromwell?

MORE: Cromwell!

WOLSEY: You'd rather do it yourself?

MORE: Me rather than Cromwell.

WOLSEY: Then come down to earth. . . . And until then, allow for an enemy, here!

MORE: As Your Grace pleases.

WOLSEY: As God wills!

MORE: Perhaps, Your Grace. (*Mounting stairs.*)

WOLSEY: More! You should have been a cleric!

MORE (*amused, looking down from gallery*): Like yourself, Your Grace?

Exit MORE. WOLSEY *is left staring, then exits through the lower arches with candle, taking most of the light from the stage as he does so. But the whole rear of the stage now patterns with webbed reflections thrown from brightly moonlit water, so that the structure is thrown into black relief, while a strip of light descends along the front of the stage, which is to be the acting area for the next scene.*

An oar and a bundle of clothing are lowered into this area from above. Enter COMMON MAN; *he unties the bundle and dons the coat and hat of* BOATMAN. Scene 3

MORE (*off*): Boat! (*Approaching.*) Boat!

BOATMAN (*donning coat and hat*): Here, sir!

MORE (*off*): A boatman please!

BOATMAN: Boat here, sir! (*He seizes the oar.*)

Enter MORE.

MORE (*peering*): Boatman?

BOATMAN: Yes, sir. (*To audience, indicating oar.*) A boatman.

MORE: Take me home.

BOATMAN (*pleasantly*): I was just going home myself, sir.

MORE: Then find me another boat.

BOATMAN: Bless you, sir – that's all right! (*Comfortably.*) I expect you'll make it worth my while, sir.

    CROMWELL *steps from behind arch, left.*

CROMWELL: Boatman, have you a licence?

BOATMAN: Eh? Bless you, sir, yes; I've got a licence.

CROMWELL: Then you know that the fares are fixed—— (*Turns to* MORE. *Exaggerated pleasure.*) Why, it's Sir Thomas!

MORE: Good morning, Master Cromwell. You work very late.

CROMWELL: I'm on my way to the Cardinal. (*He expects an answer.*)

MORE: Ah.

CROMWELL: You have just left him I think.

MORE: Yes, I have.

CROMWELL: You left him . . . in his laughing mood, I hope?

MORE: On the whole I would say, not. No, not laughing.

CROMWELL: Oh, I'm sorry. (*Backing to exit.*) I am one of your multitudinous admirers, Sir Thomas. A penny ha'penny to Chelsea, Boatman.

    Exit CROMWELL.

BOATMAN: The coming man they say, sir.

MORE: Do they? Well, where's your boat?

BOATMAN: Just along the wharf, sir.

    They are going, when enter CHAPUYS *and* ATTENDANT *from archway, Right.*

CHAPUYS: Sir Thomas More!

MORE: Signor Chapuys? You're up very late, Your Excellency.

CHAPUYS (*significantly*): So is the Cardinal, Sir Thomas.

MORE (*closing up*): He sleeps very little.

CHAPUYS: You have just left him, I think.

MORE: You are correctly informed. As always.

CHAPUYS: I will not ask you the subject of your conversation.
. . . (*He waits.*)

MORE: No, of course not.

CHAPUYS: Sir Thomas, I will be plain with you . . . plain, that
is, so far as the diplomatic decencies permit. (*Loudly.*) My
master Charles, the King of Spain! (*Pulls* MORE *aside, discreet.*) My master Charles, the King of Spain, feels himself
concerned in anything concerning his blood relation! He
would feel himself insulted by any insult offered to his father's
sister! I refer of course to Queen Catherine. (*Regards* MORE,
keenly.) The King of Spain would feel himself insulted by
any insult offered to Queen Catherine.

MORE: His feeling would be natural.

CHAPUYS (*consciously sly*): Sir Thomas, may I ask if you and
the Cardinal parted, how shall I say, amicably?

MORE: Amicably. . . . Yes.

CHAPUYS (*a shade indignant*): In agreement?

MORE: Amicably.

CHAPUYS (*warmly*): Say no more, Sir Thomas; I understand.

MORE (*a shade worried*): I hope you do, Your Excellency.

CHAPUYS: You are a good man.

MORE: I don't see how you deduce that from what I've told
you.

CHAPUYS (*holds up hand*): A nod is as good as a wink to a blind
horse. I understand. You are a good man. (*Turns to exit.*)
Dominus vobiscum.

 Exit CHAPUYS. MORE *looks after him. Then:*

MORE (*abstracted*): . . . spiritu tuo

BOATMAN (*mournful; he is squatting on the ground*): People seem
to think boats stay afloat on their own, sir, but they don't;
they cost money. (MORE *is abstractedly gazing over the
audience.*) Take anchor rope, sir, you may not believe me for
a little skiff like mine, but it's a penny a fathom. (MORE *is
still abstracted.*) And with a young wife, sir, as you know. . . .

MORE (*abstracted*): I'll pay what I always pay you. . . . The river looks very black tonight. They say it's silting up, is that so?

BOATMAN (*joining him*): Not in the middle, sir. There's a channel there getting deeper all the time.

MORE: How is your wife?

BOATMAN: She's losing her shape, sir, losing it fast.

MORE: Well, so are we all.

BOATMAN: Oh yes, sir; it's common.

MORE (*going*): Well, take me home.

Exit MORE.

BOATMAN: That I will, sir! (*Crossing to basket and pulling it out.*) From Richmond to Chelsea, downstream, a penny halfpenny . . . coat, hat . . . coat, hat (*goes for table-cloth*) from Chelsea to Richmond, upstream, a penny halfpenny. Whoever makes the regulations doesn't row a boat. Cloth. . . . (*Puts cloth in basket, takes out slippers.*) Home again.

Lighting changes to MORE'S *house interior.*

Enter MORE *on stairs. Sits wearily. Takes off hat, half takes off coat, but is too tired. It chimes three.* STEWARD *kneels to put on his slippers for him.*

MORE: Ah, Matthew. . . . Thank you. Is Lady Alice in bed?

STEWARD: Yes, sir.

MORE: Lady Margaret?

STEWARD: No, sir. Master Roper's here.

MORE (*surprised*): At this hour? . . . Who let him in?

STEWARD: He's a hard man to keep out, sir.

MORE: Where are they?

Enter MARGARET *and* ROPER.

MARGARET: Here, Father.

MORE (*regarding them, resignedly*): Good morning, William. It's a little early for breakfast.

ROPER (*solidly*): I haven't come for breakfast, sir.

MORE *looks at him and sighs.*

MARGARET: Will wants to marry me, Father.

MORE: Well, he can't marry you.

ROPER: Sir Thomas, I'm to be called to the Bar.

MORE (*warmly*): Oh, congratulations, Roper!

ROPER: My family may not be at the palace, sir, but in the City——

MORE: The Ropers were advocates when the Mores were selling pewter; there's nothing wrong with your family. There's nothing wrong with your fortune – there's nothing wrong with you – (*sourly*) except you need a clock——

ROPER: I can buy a clock, sir.

MORE: Roper, the answer's 'no'. (*Firmly.*) And will be 'no' so long as you're a heretic.

ROPER (*firing*): That's a word I don't like, Sir Thomas!

MORE: It's not a likeable word. (*Coming to life.*) It's not a likeable thing!

> MARGARET *is alarmed, and from behind* MORE *tries to silence* ROPER.

ROPER: The Church is heretical! Doctor Luther's proved that to my satisfaction!

MORE: Luther's an excommunicate.

ROPER: From a heretic Church! Church? It's a shop—— Forgiveness by the florin! Joblots now in Germany!... Mmm, and divorces.

MORE (*expressionless*): Divorces?

ROPER: Oh, half England's buzzing with that.

MORE: 'Half England.' The Inns of Court may be buzzing, England doesn't buzz so easily.

ROPER: It will. And is that a Church? Is that a Cardinal? Is that a Pope? Or Antichrist! (MORE *looks up angrily.* MARGARET *signals frantically.*) Look, what I know I'll say!

MARGARET: You've no sense of the *place*!

MORE (*rueful*): He's no sense of the time.

ROPER: I—— (*But* MORE *gently holds up his hand and he stops.*)

MORE: Listen, Roper. Two years ago you were a passionate Churchman; now you're a passionate – Lutheran. We must just pray, that when your head's finished turning your face is to the front again.

ROPER: Don't lengthen your prayers with *me*, sir!

MORE: Oh, one more or less. . . . Is your horse here?

ROPER: No, I walked.

MORE: Well, take a horse from the stables and get back home. (ROPER *hesitates*.) Go along.

ROPER: May I come again? (MORE *indicates* MARGARET.)

MARGARET: Yes. Soon.

ROPER: Good night, sir.

Exit ROPER.

MARGARET: Is that final, Father?

MORE: As long as he's a heretic, Meg, that's absolute. (*Warmly*.) Nice boy. . . . Terribly strong principles though. I told you to go to bed.

MARGARET: Yes, why?

MORE (*lightly*): Because I intended you to *go* to bed. You're very pensive?

MARGARET: You're very gay. Did he talk about the divorce?

MORE: Mm? You know I think we've been on the wrong track with Will—— It's no good arguing with a Roper——

MARGARET: Father, did he?

MORE: *Old* Roper was just the same. Now let him think he's going *with* the current and he'll turn round and start swimming in the opposite direction. What we want is a really substantial attack on the Church.

MARGARET: We're going to get it, aren't we?

MORE: Margaret, I'll not have you talk treason. . . . And I'll not have you repeat lawyer's gossip. I'm a lawyer myself and I know what it's worth.

ALICE (*off. Indignant and excited*): Thomas——!

MORE: Now look what you've done.

Enter ALICE *at head of stairs in nightgown.*

ALICE: Young Roper! I've just seen young Roper! On *my* horse.

MORE: He'll bring it back, dear. He's been to see Margaret.

ALICE: Oh – why you don't beat that girl!

MORE: No no, she's full of education – and it's a delicate commodity.

ALICE: Mm! And more's the pity!

MORE: Yes, but it's there now and think what it cost. (*He sneezes.*)

ALICE (*pouncing*): Ah! Margaret – hot water.

    Exit MARGARET.

MORE: I'm sorry you were awakened, chick.

ALICE: I wasn't sleeping very deeply, Thomas – what did Wolsey want?

MORE (*innocent*): Young Roper asked for Margaret.

ALICE: What! Impudence!

MORE: Yes, wasn't it?

ALICE: Old fox! What did he want, Thomas?

MORE: He wanted me to read a dispatch.

ALICE: Was that all?

MORE: A Latin dispatch.

ALICE: Oh! Won't you talk about it?

MORE (*gently*): No.

    Enter MARGARET *with cup which she takes to* MORE.

ALICE: Norfolk was speaking for you as Chancellor before he left.

MORE: He's a dangerous friend then. Wolsey's Chancellor, God help him. We don't want another. (MARGARET *takes cup to him; he sniffs it.*) I don't want this.

ALICE: Drink it. Great men get colds in the head just the same as commoners.

MORE: That's dangerous, levelling talk, Alice. Beware of the Tower. (*Rises.*) I will, I'll drink it in bed.

    All move to stairs and ascend, talking.

MARGARET: Would you want to be Chancellor?

MORE: No.

MARGARET: That's what I said. But Norfolk said if Wolsey fell——

MORE (*no longer flippant*): If Wolsey fell, the splash would swamp a few small boats like ours. There will be no new Chancellors while Wolsey lives.

Scene 5 *Exit above.*

The light is dimmed there and a bright spot descends below. Into this bright circle from the wings is thrown the great red robe and the Cardinal's hat. The COMMON MAN *enters from the opposite wing and roughly piles them into his basket. He then takes from his pocket a pair of spectacles and from the basket a book. He reads:*

COMMON MAN (*reading*): 'Whether we follow tradition in ascribing Wolsey's death to a broken heart, or accept Professor Larcomb's less feeling diagnosis of pulmonary pneumonia, its effective cause was the King's displeasure. He died at Leicester on 29 November 1530 while on his way to the Tower under charge of High Treason.

'England's next Lord Chancellor was Sir Thomas More, a scholar and, by popular repute, a saint. His scholarship is supported by his writings; saintliness is a quality less easy to establish. But from his wilful indifference to realities which were obvious to quite ordinary contemporaries, it seems all too probable that he had it.'

Exit COMMON MAN. *As he goes, lights come up and a screen is lowered depicting Hampton Court.* CROMWELL *is sitting half-way up the stairs.*

Enter RICH, *crossing.*

CROMWELL: Rich! (RICH *stops, sees him, and smiles willingly.*) What brings you to Hampton?

RICH: I came with the Duke last night, Master Cromwell. They're hunting again.

CROMWELL: It's a kingly pastime, Master Rich. (*Both smile.*) I'm glad you found employment. You're the Duke's Secretary are you not?

RICH (*flustered*): My work *is* mostly secretarial.

CROMWELL (*as one making an effort of memory*): Or is it his librarian you are?

RICH: I do look after His Grace's library, yes.

CROMWELL: Oh. Well, that's something. And I don't suppose you're bothered much by His Grace – in the library? (RICH *smiles uncertainly*.) It's odd how differently men's fortunes flow. My late master died in disgrace, and here I am in the King's own service. There you are in a *comparative* backwater – yet the new Lord Chancellor's an old friend of yours. (*He looks at him directly.*)

RICH (*uncertainly*): He isn't really my *friend*. . . .

CROMWELL: Oh, I thought he was. (*Gets up, prepares to go.*)

RICH: – In a sense he is.

CROMWELL (*reproachful*): Well, I always understood he set you up in life.

RICH: Master Cromwell – what *is* it that you do for the King? *Enter* CHAPUYS.

CHAPUYS (*roguish*): Yes, *I* should like to know that, Master Cromwell. *not a specific title*

CROMWELL: Ah, Signor Chapuys. You've met His Excellency Rich? (*Indicates* CHAPUYS.) The Spanish Ambassador. (*Indicates* RICH.) The Duke of Norfolk's librarian.

CHAPUYS: But how should we introduce *you*, Master Cromwell, if we had the happiness?

CROMWELL: Oh sly! Do you notice how sly he is, Rich? (*Walks away.*) Well, I suppose you would call me (*suddenly turns*) 'The King's Ear'. . . . (*Deprecating shrug.*) It's a useful organ, the ear. But in fact it's even simpler than that. When the King wants something done, I do it.

CHAPUYS: Ah. (*Mock interest.*) But then why these Justices, Chancellors, Admirals?

CROMWELL: Oh, *they* are the constitution. Our ancient, English constitution. I merely do things. *disregard*

CHAPUYS: For example, Master Cromwell. . . .

CROMWELL (*admiring*): Oho – beware these professional diplomats. Well now, for example; next week at Deptford we are launching the *Great Harry* – one thousand tons, four masts, sixty-six guns, an overall length of one hundred and seventy-five feet, it's expected to be very effective – all this you probably know. However you may not know that the King himself will guide her down the river; yes, the King himself will be her pilot. He will have assistance of course but he himself will be her pilot. He will have a pilot's whistle upon which he will blow, and he will wear in every respect a common pilot's uniform. Except for the material, which will be cloth of gold. These innocent fancies require more preparation than you might suppose and someone has to do it. (*He spreads his hands.*) Meanwhile, I do prepare myself for, higher things. I stock my mind.

CHAPUYS: Alas, Master Cromwell, don't we all? This ship for instance – it has fifty-six guns by the way, not sixty-six and only forty of them heavy—— After the launching I understand, the King will take his barge to Chelsea. (CROMWELL'S *face darkens during this speech.*)

CROMWELL (*sharply*): Yes——

CHAPUYS: – To——

CROMWELL ⎱
CHAPUYS ⎰ (*together*): Sir Thomas More's.

CHAPUYS (*sweetly*): Will you be there?

CROMWELL: Oh no – they'll talk about the divorce. (*It is* CHAPUYS' *turn to be shocked:* RICH *draws away uneasily.*) The King will ask him for an answer.

CHAPUYS (*ruffled*): He has given his answer!

CROMWELL: The King will ask him for another.

CHAPUYS: Sir Thomas is a good son of the Church!

CROMWELL: Sir Thomas is a man.

Enter STEWARD. *Both* CROMWELL *and* CHAPUYS *look towards him sharply, then back at one another.*

CHAPUYS (*innocently*): Isn't that his Steward now?

CROMWELL: I believe it is. Well, good day, Your Excellency.

CHAPUYS (*eager*): Good day, Master Cromwell. (*He expects him to go.*)

CROMWELL (*standing firm*): Good day. (*And* CHAPUYS *has to go.*)

 CROMWELL *walks side stage, with furtive and urgent beckonings to* STEWARD *to follow.* RICH *follows but hangs off. Meanwhile* CHAPUYS *and his* ATTENDANT *have gone behind screen, beneath which their legs protrude clearly.*

STEWARD (*conspiratorial*): Sir, Sir Thomas doesn't talk about it. (*He waits but* CROMWELL *remains stony.*) He doesn't talk about it, to his wife, sir. (*He waits again.*)

CROMWELL: This is worth nothing.

STEWARD (*significant*): But he doesn't talk about it to Lady Margaret – that's his daughter, sir.

CROMWELL: So?

STEWARD: So he's worried, sir. . . (CROMWELL *is interested.*) Frightened. . . . (CROMWELL *takes out a coin but pauses suspiciously.*) Sir, he goes *white* when it's mentioned!

CROMWELL (*hands coin*): All right.

STEWARD (*looks at coin; reproachful*): Oh, sir——!

CROMWELL (*waves him away*): Are you coming in my direction, Rich? *are you on my side*

RICH (*still hanging off*): No no.

CROMWELL: I think you should, you know.

RICH: *I* can't tell you anything!

 Exit RICH *and* CROMWELL *left and right.* CHAPUYS *and* ATTENDANT *come from behind screen.*

CHAPUYS (*beckons* STEWARD): Well?

STEWARD: Sir Thomas rises at six, sir, and prays for an hour and a half.

CHAPUYS: Yes?

STEWARD: During Lent, sir, he lived entirely on bread and water.

CHAPUYS: Yes?

STEWARD: He goes to confession twice a week, sir. Parish priest. Dominican.

CHAPUYS: Ah. He is a true son of the Church.

STEWARD (*soapy*): That he is, sir.

CHAPUYS: What did Master Cromwell want?

STEWARD: Same as you, sir.

CHAPUYS: No man can serve two masters, Steward.

STEWARD: No indeed, sir; I serve one. (*He pulls to the front an enormous cross until then hanging at his back on a length of string – a caricature of the ebony cross worn by* CHAPUYS.)

CHAPUYS: Good, simple man. Here. (*Gives coin. Going.*) Peace be with you.

STEWARD: And with you, sir.

CHAPUYS: Our Lord watch you.

STEWARD: You too, sir. (*Exit* CHAPUYS.) That's a very religious man.

    Enter RICH.

RICH: What does Signor Chapuys want, Matthew?

STEWARD: I've no idea, sir.

RICH (*gives coin*): What did you tell him?

STEWARD: I told him that Sir Thomas says his prayers and goes to confession.

RICH: Why that?

STEWARD: That's what he wanted to know, sir. I mean I could have told him any number of things about Sir Thomas – that he has rheumatism, prefers red wine to white, is easily sea-sick, fond of kippers, afraid of drowning. But that's what he wanted to know, sir.

RICH: What did he say?

STEWARD: He said that Sir Thomas is a good churchman, sir.

RICH (*going*): Well, that's true, isn't it?

STEWARD: I'm just telling you what he said, sir. Master Cromwell went that way, sir.

RICH (*furious*): Did I ask you which way Master Cromwell went?

    Exit RICH *opposite.*

STEWARD (*to audience, thoughtfully*): The great thing's not to get out of your depth. . . . What I can tell them's common

knowledge! But now they've given money for it and everyone wants value for his money. They'll make a secret of it
now to prove they've not been bilked. . . . They'll make it
a secret by making it dangerous. . . . Mm. . . . Oh, when I
can't touch the bottom I'll go deaf, blind and dumb. (*Holds
out coins.*) And that's more than I *earn* in a fortnight!

*On this; a fanfare of trumpets; plainsong; the rear of the stage
becomes a source of glittering blue light; Hampton Court is hoisted
out of sight, and other screens are lowered one after the other, each
masking the rest, bearing respectively sunflowers, hollyhocks, roses,
magnolias. When the fanfare ceases the plainsong goes on quietly,
and the screens throw long shadows like the shadows of trees, and*
NORFOLK, ALICE, MARGARET, *erupt on to the stage.*

ALICE (*distressed*): No sign of him, my lord!

NORFOLK: God's body, Alice, he must be found!

ALICE (*to* MEG): He *must* be in the house!

MARGARET: He's *not* in the house, Mother!

ALICE: Then he must be here in the garden!

They 'search' among the screens.

NORFOLK: He takes things too far, Alice.

ALICE: Do I not know it?

NORFOLK: It will end badly for him!

ALICE: I know that too!

They 'notice' the STEWARD.

MARGARET ⎫   ⎫ Matthew! Where's my father?
ALICE   ⎬ (*together*): ⎨ Where is Sir Thomas?
NORFOLK ⎭   ⎭ Where's your master?

Fanfare, shorter but nearer.

NORFOLK (*despairing*): Oh my God.

ALICE: Oh Jesus!

STEWARD: My lady – the King?

NORFOLK: Yes, fool! (*Threatening.*) And if the King arrives
and the Chancellor's not here——

STEWARD: Sir, my lady, it's not *my* fault!

NORFOLK (*quietly displeased*): Lady Alice, Thomas'll get no good of it. This is not how Wolsey made himself great.

ALICE (*stiffly*): Thomas has his own way of doing things, my lord!

NORFOLK (*testy*): Yes yes, Thomas is unique; but where *is* Thomas?

    STEWARD *swings onstage small gothic door. Plainsong. All run to the door.* NORFOLK *opens it.*

ALICE: Thomas!

STEWARD: Sir!

MARGARET: Father!

NORFOLK (*indignant*): My Lord Chancellor!

    Enter MORE *through the doorway. He blinks in the light. He is wearing a cassock. Shuts door behind him.*

What sort of fooling is this? Does the King visit you every day.

MORE: No, but I go to Vespers most days.

NORFOLK: He's here!

MORE: But isn't this visit *meant* to be a surprise?

NORFOLK (*grimly*): For you, yes, not for him.

MARGARET: Father. . . . (*Indicates cassock.*)

NORFOLK: Yes – d'you propose to meet the King disguised as a parish clerk? (*They fall upon him and drag the cassock over his head.*) A parish clerk, my lord Chancellor! You dishonour the King and his office!

MORE (*appearing momentarily in the folds of the cassock*): The service of God is not a dishonour to any office. (*The cassock is pulled off.*) Believe me, my friend, I do not belittle the honour His Majesty is doing me. (*Briskly.*) Well! That's a lovely dress, Alice; so's that, Margaret. (*Looks at* NORFOLK.) I'm a dowdy bird, aren't I? (*Looks at* ALICE.) Calm yourself, Alice, we're all ready now.

    He turns about and we see that his gown is caught up behind him revealing his spindly legs in long hose laced up at the thighs.

ALICE: Thomas!

    MARGARET *laughs.*

MORE: What's the matter? (*Turns round again and his women folk pursue him to pull down the gown while* NORFOLK *throws his hands in the air. Expostulation, explanation, exclamation, overlapping in a babble.*)

NORFOLK: – By God you can be hare-brained——!

MARGARET: – Be still——!

ALICE: – Oh, Thomas! Thomas!——

NORFOLK: – What whim possessed you——

MORE: – 'Twas not a whim——!

ALICE: – Your second best stockings——!

MARGARET: – Father, be still——!

NORFOLK: – Oh, enough's enough——!

MORE: – Haven't you done——!

    HENRY, *in a cloth of gold, runs out of the sunlight half-way down the steps, and blows a blast on his pilot's whistle. All kneel. In the silence he descends slowly to their level, blowing softly . . .*

MORE: Your Majesty does my house more honour than I fear my household can bear.

HENRY: No ceremony, Thomas! No ceremony! (*They rise.*) A passing fancy – I happened to be on the river. (*Holds out shoe, proudly.*) Look, mud.

MORE: We do it in better style, Your Grace, when we come by the road.

HENRY: Oh, the road! There's the road for me, Thomas, the river; *my* river. . . . By heaven what an evening! I fear we come upon you unexpectedly, Lady Alice.

ALICE (*shocked*): Oh no, Your Grace – (*remembering*) that is yes, but we are ready for you – ready to entertain Your Grace that is.

MORE: This is my daughter Margaret, sir. She has not had the honour to meet Your Grace. (*She curtseys low.*)

HENRY (*looks her over, then*): Why, Margaret, they told me you were a scholar.

    MARGARET *is confused.*

MORE: Answer, Margaret.

MARGARET: Among women I pass for one Your Grace. (NORFOLK *and* ALICE *exchange approving glances.*)

HENRY: Antiquone modo Latine loqueris, an Oxoniensi? [Is your Latin the old Latin, or Oxford Latin?]

MARGARET: Quem me docuit pater, Domine. [My father's Latin, Sire.]

HENRY: Bene. Optimus est. Graecamne linguam quoque te docuit? [Good. That is the best. And has he taught you Greek too?]

MARGARET: Graecam me docuit non pater meus sed mei patris amicus, Johannes Coletus, Sancti Pauli Decanus. In litteris Graecis tamen, non minus quam Latinis, ars magistri minuitur discipuli stultitia.

[Not my father, Sire, but my father's friend, John Colet, Dean of St Paul's. But it is with the Greek as it is with the Latin; the skill of the master is lost in the pupil's lack of it.]

Her Latin is better than his; he is not altogether pleased.

HENRY: Ho! (*He walks away from her, talking; she begins to rise from her curtsey,* MORE *gently presses her down again before the King turns.*) Take care, Thomas: 'There is no end to the making of books and too much reading is a weariness of the flesh.' (*Back to* MARGARET.) Can you dance, too?

MARGARET: Not well, Your Grace.

HENRY: Well, *I* dance superlatively! (*Plants his leg before her face.*) That's a dancer's *leg*, Margaret! (*She has the wit to look straight up and smile at him. All good humour he pulls her to her feet; sees* NORFOLK *grinning the grin of a comrade.*) Hey, Norfolk? (*Indicates* NORFOLK's *leg with much distaste.*) Now *that's* a wrestler's leg. But I can throw him. (*Seizes* NORFOLK.) Shall I show them, Howard? (NORFOLK *is alarmed for his dignity. To* MARGARET.) Shall I?

MARGARET (*looking at* NORFOLK, *gently*): No, Your Grace.

HENRY (*releases* NORFOLK, *seriously*): You are gentle. (*To* MORE, *approving.*) That's good. (*To* MARGARET.) You shall read to me. (MARGARET *is about to demur.*) No no, you shall read to me. Lady Alice, the river's given me an appetite.

ALICE: If Your Grace would share a very simple supper.

HENRY: It would please me to. (*Preparing to lead off, sees* MARGARET *again.*) I'm something of a scholar too; did you know?

MARGARET: All the world knows Your Grace's Book, asserting the seven sacraments of the Church.

HENRY: Ah yes. Between ourselves, your father had a hand in that; eh, Thomas?

MORE: Here and there, Your Grace. In a minor capacity.

HENRY (*looking at him*): He seeks to shame me with his modesty. . . . (*Turns to* ALICE.) On second thoughts we'll follow, Lady Alice, Thomas and I will follow. (*He waves them off. They bow, withdraw, prepare for second bow.*) Wait! (*Raises whistle to lips; then:*) Margaret, are you fond of music?

MARGARET: Yes, Your Grace.

HENRY (*beckons her to him; holds out whistle*): Blow. (*She is uncertain.*) Blow. (*She does.*) Louder! (*She does and at once music without, stately and oversweet. Expressions of pleasure all round.*) I brought them with me, Lady Alice; take them in! (*Exit all but* MORE *and* HENRY. *The music continues receding.*) Listen to this, Thomas. (*He walks about, the auditor, beating time.*) Do you know it?

MORE: No, Your Grace, I——

HENRY: Sh! (MORE *is silent;* HENRY *goes on with his listening.*) . . . I launched a ship today, Thomas.

MORE: Yes, Your Grace, I——

HENRY: *Listen*, man, listen. . . . (*A silence.*) . . . The *Great Harry* . . . I steered her, Thomas, under sail.

MORE: You have many accomplishments, Your Grace.

HENRY (*holds up a finger for silence. . . . A silence*): A great experience. (MORE *keeps silent.*) . . . A great experience, Thomas.

MORE: Yes, Your Grace.

The music is growing fainter.

HENRY: I am a fool.

MORE: How so, Your Grace?

HENRY (*a silence, during which the music fades to silence*): . . . What else but a fool to live in a Court, in a licentious mob – when I have friends, with gardens.

MORE: Your Grace——

HENRY: No courtship, no ceremony, Thomas. Be seated. You *are* my friend are you not? (MORE *sits*.)

MORE: Your Majesty.

HENRY: And thank God I have a friend for my Chancellor. (*Laughing*.) Readier to be friends I trust than he was to be Chancellor.

MORE: My own knowledge of my poor abilities——

HENRY: I will judge of your abilities, Thomas. . . . Did you know that Wolsey named you for Chancellor?

MORE: Wolsey!

HENRY: Aye; before he died. Wolsey named you and Wolsey was no fool.

MORE: He was a statesman of incomparable ability, Your Grace.

HENRY: Was he? Was he so? (*Rises*.) Then why did he fail me? Be seated – it was villainy then! Yes villainy. I was right to break him; he was all pride, Thomas; a proud man; pride right through. And he failed me! (MORE *opens his mouth*.) He failed me in the one thing that mattered! The one thing that matters, Thomas, then or now. And why? He wanted to be Pope! Yes, he wanted to be the Bishop of Rome. I'll tell you something, Thomas, and you can check this for yourself – it was never merry in England while we had Cardinals amongst us. (*He nods significantly at* MORE *who lowers his eyes*.) But look now – (*walking away*) – I shall forget the feel of that . . . great tiller under my hands . . . I took her down to Dogget's Bank, went about and brought her up in Tilbury Roads. A man could sail clean round the world in that ship.

MORE (*affectionate admiration*): Some men could, Your Grace.

HENRY (*off-hand*): Touching this matter of my divorce, Thomas; have you thought of it since we last talked?

MORE: Of little else.

HENRY: Then you see your way clear to me?

MORE: That you should put away Queen Catherine, sire? Oh, alas (*thumps table in distress*), as I think of it I see so clearly that I can *not* come with Your Grace that my endeavour is not to think of it at all.

HENRY: Then you have not thought enough! . . . (*With real appeal.*) Great God, Thomas, why do you hold out against me in the desire of my heart – the very wick of my heart?——

MORE (*draws up sleeve, baring his arm*): There is my right arm. (*A practical proposition.*) Take your dagger and saw it from my shoulder, and I will laugh and be thankful, if by that means I can come with Your Grace with a clear conscience.

HENRY (*uncomfortably pulls at the sleeve*): I know it, Thomas, I know. . . .

MORE (*rises, formally*): I crave pardon if I offend.

HENRY (*suspiciously*): Speak then.

MORE: When I took the Great Seal your Majesty promised not to pursue me on this matter.

HENRY: Ha! So I break my word, Master More! No no, I'm joking . . . I joke roughly. . . . (*Wanders away.*) I often think I'm a rough fellow. . . . Yes, a rough young fellow. (*Shakes his head indulgently.*) Be seated. . . . That's a magnolia. We have one like it at Hampton – not so red as that though. Ha – I'm in an excellent frame of mind. (*Glances at the magnolia.*) Beautiful. (*Reasonable, pleasant.*) You must consider, Thomas, that I stand in peril of my soul. It was no marriage; she was my brother's widow. Leviticus: 'Thou shalt not uncover the nakedness of thy brother's wife.' Leviticus, Chapter 18, Verse 16.

MORE: Yes, Your Grace. But Deuteronomy——

HENRY (*triumphant*): Deuteronomy's ambiguous!

MORE (*bursting out*): Your Grace, I'm not fit to meddle in these matters – to me it seems a matter for the Holy See——

HENRY (*reproving*): Thomas, Thomas, does a man need a Pope to tell him when he's sinned? It was a sin, Thomas; I admit it; I repent. And God has punished me; I have no son. . . . Son after son she's borne me, Thomas, all dead at birth, or dead within the month; I never saw the hand of God so clear in anything. . . . I have a daughter, she's a good child, a well-set child—— But I have no son. (*Flares up.*) It is my bounden *duty* to put away the Queen and all the Popes back to St Peter shall not come between me and my duty! How is it that you cannot see? Everyone else does.

MORE (*eagerly*): Then why does Your Grace need my poor support?

HENRY: Because you are honest. What's more to the purpose, you're known to be honest. . . . There are those like Norfolk who follow me because I wear the crown, and there are those like Master Cromwell who follow me because they are jackals with sharp teeth and I am their lion, and there is a mass that follows me because it follows anything that moves – and there is you.

MORE: I am sick to think how much I must displease Your Grace.

HENRY: No, Thomas, I respect your sincerity. Respect? Oh, man it's water in the desert. . . . How did you like our music? That air they played, it had a certain – well, tell me what you thought of it.

MORE (*relieved at this turn; smiling*): Could it have been Your Grace's own?

HENRY (*smiles back*): Discovered! Now I'll never know your true opinion. And that's irksome, Thomas, for we artists, though we love praise, yet we love truth better.

MORE (*mildly*): Then I will tell Your Grace truly what I thought of it.

HENRY (*a little disconcerted*): Speak then.

MORE: To me it seemed – delightful. *wisdom*

HENRY: Thomas – I chose the right man for Chancellor.

MORE: I must in fairness add that my taste in music is reputedly deplorable.

HENRY: Your taste in music is excellent. It exactly coincides with my own. Ah music! Music! Send them back without me, Thomas; I will live here in Chelsea and make music.

MORE: My house is at Your Grace's disposal.

HENRY: Thomas, you understand me; we will stay here together and make music.

MORE: Will your Grace honour my roof at dinner?

HENRY (*has walked away, blowing moodily on his whistle*): Mm? Yes; I expect I'll bellow for you. . . .

MORE: My wife will be more——

HENRY: Yes, yes. (*He turns, his face set.*) Touching this other business, mark you, Thomas, I'll have no opposition.

MORE (*sadly*): Your Grace?

HENRY: No opposition I say! No opposition! Your conscience is your own affair; but you are my Chancellor! There, you have my word – I'll leave you out of it. But I don't take it kindly, Thomas, and I'll have no opposition! I see how it will be; the Bishops will oppose me. The full-fed, hypocritical, 'Princes of the *Church*'! Ha! As for the Pope! – Am I to burn in Hell because the Bishop of Rome with the Emperor's knife to his throat, mouths me Deuteronomy? Hypocrites! They're all hypocrites! Mind they do not take you in, Thomas! Lie low if you will, but I'll brook no opposition – no words, no signs, no letters, no pamphlets – mind that, Thomas – no writings against me!

MORE: Your Grace is unjust. I am Your Grace's loyal minister. If I cannot serve Your Grace in this great matter of the Queen——

HENRY: I have no Queen! Catherine is not my wife and no priest can make her so, and they that say she is my wife are not only liars . . . but Traitors! Mind it, Thomas!

MORE: Am I a babbler, Your Grace? (*But his voice is unsteady.*)

HENRY: You are stubborn. . . . (*Wooingly.*) If you could come with me, you are the man I would soonest raise – yes, with my own hand.

MORE (*covers his face*): Oh, Your Grace overwhelms me!
  A complicated chiming of little bells is heard.

HENRY: What's that?

MORE: Eight o'clock, Your Grace.

HENRY (*uneasily eyeing* MORE): Oh, lift yourself up, man – have I not promised? (MORE *braces.*) Shall we eat?

MORE: If Your Grace pleases. (*Recovering.*) What will Your Grace sing for us? (*They approach the stairs.*)

HENRY: Eight o'clock you said? Thomas, the tide will be changing. I was forgetting the tide. I'd better go.

MORE (*gravely*): I'm sorry, Your Grace.

HENRY: I must catch the tide or I'll not get back to Richmond till. . . . No, don't come. Tell Norfolk. (*He has his foot on the bottom stair when enter* ALICE *and* STEWARD *above.*) Oh, Lady Alice, I must go. (ALICE *descends, her face serious.*) I want to catch the tide. To tell the truth, Lady Alice, I have forgotten in your haven here how time flows past outside. Affairs call me to court and so I give you my thanks and say Good night.
  (*He mounts.*)

MORE ⎫
ALICE ⎭ (*bowing*): Good night, Your Grace.

  Exit HENRY, *above.*

ALICE: What's this? You crossed him.

MORE: Somewhat.

ALICE: Why?

MORE (*apologetic*): I couldn't find the other way.

ALICE (*angrily*): You're too nice altogether, Thomas!

MORE: Woman, mind your house.

ALICE: I *am* minding my house!

MORE *(takes in her anxiety)*: Well, Alice. What would you *want* me to do?

ALICE: Be ruled! If you won't rule him, be ruled!

MORE *(quietly)*: I neither could nor would rule my King. *(Pleasantly.)* But there's a little . . . little, area . . . where I must rule myself. It's very little – less to him than a tennis court. *(Her face is still full of foreboding: he sighs.)* Look; it was eight o'clock. At eight o'clock, Lady Anne likes to dance.

ALICE *(relieved)*: Oh?

MORE: I think so.

ALICE *(irritation)*: And *you* stand between them!

MORE: I? What stands between them is a sacrament of the Church. I'm less important than you think, Alice.

ALICE *(appealing)*: Thomas, stay friends with him.

MORE: Whatever can be done by smiling, you may rely on me to do.

ALICE: You don't know *how* to flatter.

MORE: I flatter very well! My recipe's beginning to be widely copied. It's the basic syrup with just a soupçon of discreet impudence. . . .

ALICE *(still uneasy)*: I wish he'd eaten here. . . .

MORE: Yes – we shall be living on that 'simple supper' of yours for a fortnight. *(She won't laugh.)* Alice. . . . *(She won't turn.)* Alice. . . . *(She turns.)* Set your mind at rest – this *(tapping himself)* is not the stuff of which martyrs are made.

   Enter above, quickly, ROPER.

ROPER: Sir Thomas!

MORE *(winces)*: Oh, no. . . !

ALICE: Will Roper, what d'you want?

   Enter after ROPER, MARGARET.

MARGARET: William, I told you not to!

ROPER: I'm not easily 'told', Meg.

MARGARET: I *asked* you not to.

ROPER: Meg, I'm full to here! *(Indicates throat.)*

MARGARET: It's not convenient!

ROPER: Must everything be made convenient? I'm not a convenient man, Meg – I've got an inconvenient conscience!

MARGARET *gestures helplessly to* MORE.

MORE (*laughs*): Joshua's trumpet. One note on that brass conscience of yours and my daughter's walls are down.

ROPER (*descending*): You raised her, sir.

MORE (*a bit puzzled*): How long have you been here? Are you in the King's party?

ROPER: No, sir, I am *not* in the King's party! (*Advancing.*) It's of that I wish to speak to you. My spirit is perturbed.

MORE (*suppressing a grin*): Is it, Will? Why?

ROPER: I've been offered a seat in the next Parliament. (MORE *looks up sharply.*) Ought I to take it?

MORE: No ... Well that depends. With your views on Church Reformation I should have thought you could do yourself a lot of good in the next Parliament.

ROPER: My views on the Church – I must confess—— Since last we met my views have somewhat modified. (MORE *and* MARGARET *exchange a smile.*) I modify nothing concerning the *body* of the Church – the money-changers in the temple must be scourged from thence – with a scourge of fire if that is needed! ... But an attack on the Church herself! No, I see behind that an attack on God——

MORE: – Roper——

ROPER: The Devil's work!

MORE: – Roper——!

ROPER: To be done by the Devil's ministers!

MORE: For heaven's sake remember my office!

ROPER: Oh, if you stand on your office——

MORE: I don't stand on it, but there are certain things I may not hear!

ROPER: Sophistication. It is what I was told. The Court has corrupted you, Sir Thomas; you are not the man you were; you have learnt to study your 'convenience'; you have learnt to flatter!

MORE: There, Alice; you see? I have a reputation for it.

ALICE: God's Body, young man, if I was the Chancellor I'd have you whipped!

Enter STEWARD.

STEWARD: Master Rich is here, Sir Thomas.

RICH *follows him closely.*

RICH: Good evening, sir.

MORE: Ah, Richard?

RICH: Good evening, Lady Alice. (ALICE *nods, non-committal.*) Lady Margaret.

MARGARET (*quite friendly but very clear*): Good evening, Master Rich.

A pause.

MORE: Do you know——? (*Indicates* ROPER.) William Roper, the younger.

RICH: By reputation, of course.

ROPER: Good evening, Master . . .

RICH: Rich.

ROPER: Oh. (*Recollecting something.*) Oh.

RICH (*quick and hostile*): You have heard of me?

ROPER (*shortly*): Yes.

RICH (*excitedly*): In what connection? I don't know what you can have heard—— (*Looks about: hotly.*) I sense that I'm not welcome here! (*He has jumped the gun; they are startled.*)

MORE (*gently*): Why, Richard, have you done something that should make you not welcome?

RICH: Why, do you suspect me of it?

MORE: I shall begin to.

RICH (*draws closer to him and speaks hurriedly*): Cromwell is asking questions. About you. About you particularly. (MORE *is unmoved.*) He is continually collecting information about you!

MORE: I know it. (STEWARD *begins to slide out.*) Stay a minute, Matthew.

RICH (*pointing*): *That's* one of his sources!

MORE: Of course; that's one of my servants.

RICH (*hurried, low voice again*): Signor Chapuys, the Imperial Ambassador——

MORE – Collects information too. That's one of his functions. (*He looks at* RICH *very gravely.*)

RICH (*voice cracking*): You look at me as though I were an enemy!

MORE (*puts out a hand to steady him*): Why, Richard, you're shaking.

RICH: I'm adrift. Help me.

MORE: How?

RICH: Employ me.

MORE: No.

RICH (*desperately*): Employ me!

MORE: No!

RICH (*moves swiftly to exit: turns there*): I would be steadfast!

MORE: Richard, you couldn't answer for yourself even so far as tonight.

    Exit RICH. *All watch him; the others turn to* MORE, *their faces alert.*

ROPER: Arrest him.

ALICE: Yes!

MORE: For what?

ALICE: He's dangerous!

ROPER: For libel; he's a spy.

ALICE: He is! Arrest him!

MARGARET: Father, that man's bad.

MORE: There is no law against that.

ROPER: There is! God's law!

MORE: Then God can arrest him.

ROPER: Sophistication upon sophistication!

MORE: No, sheer simplicity. The law, Roper, the law. I know what's legal not what's right. And I'll stick to what's legal.

ROPER: Then you set Man's law above God's!

MORE: No far below; but let me draw your attention to a

fact – I'm *not* God. The currents and eddies of right and wrong, which you find such plain-sailing, I can't navigate, I'm no voyager. But in the thickets of the law, oh there I'm a forester. I doubt if there's a man alive who could follow me there, thank God. . . . (*He says this to himself.*)

ALICE (*exasperated, pointing after* RICH): While you talk, he's gone!

MORE: And go he should if he was the devil himself until he broke the law!

ROPER: So now you'd give the Devil benefit of law!

MORE: Yes. What would you do? Cut a great road through the law to get after the Devil?

ROPER: I'd cut down every law in England to do that!

MORE (*roused and excited*): Oh? (*Advances on* ROPER.) And when the last law was down, and the Devil turned round on you – where would you hide, Roper, the laws all being flat? (*Leaves him.*) This country's planted thick with laws from coast to coast – Man's laws, not God's – and if you cut them down – and you're just the man to do it – d'you really think you could stand upright in the winds that would blow then? (*Quietly.*) Yes, I'd give the Devil benefit of law, for my own safety's sake.

ROPER: I have long suspected this; this is the golden calf; the law's your god.

MORE (*wearily*): Oh, Roper, you're a fool, God's my god. . . . (*Rather bitter.*) But I find him rather too (*very bitter*) subtle . . . I don't know where he is nor what he wants.

ROPER: My god wants service, to the end and unremitting; nothing else!

MORE (*dry*): Are you sure that's God? – He sounds like Moloch. But indeed it may be God—— And whoever hunts for me, Roper, God or Devil, will find me hiding in the thickets of the law! And I'll hide my daughter with me! Not hoist her up the mainmast of your seagoing principles! They put about too nimbly!

Exit MORE. *They all look after him.* MARGARET *touches* ROPER'S *hand.*

MARGARET: Oh, that was harsh.

ROPER (*turning to her, serious*): What's happened here?

ALICE (*still with her back to them, her voice strained*): He can't abide a fool, that's all! Be off!

ROPER (*to* MARGARET): Hide you. Hide you from what?

ALICE (*turning, near to tears*): He said nothing about hiding me you noticed! I've got too fat to hide I suppose!

MARGARET: You know he meant us both.

ROPER: But from what?

ALICE: I don't know. I don't know if he knows. He's not said one simple, direct word to me since this divorce came up. It's not God who's gone subtle! It's him!

Enter MORE, *a little sheepish. Goes to* ROPER.

MORE (*kindly*): Roper, that was harsh: your principles are – (*can't resist sending him up*) excellent – the very best quality. (ROPER *bridles. Contrite.*) No truly now, your principles are fine. (*Indicating stairs, to all.*) Look, we must make a start on all that food.

MARGARET: Father, can't you be plain with us?

MORE (*looks quickly from daughter to wife. Takes* ALICE'S *hand.*) I stand on the wrong side of no statute, and no common law. (*Takes* MEG'S *hand too.*) I have not disobeyed my sovereign. I truly believe no man in England is safer than myself. And I want my supper. (*He starts them up the stairs and goes to* ROPER.) We shall need your assistance, Will. There's an excellent Burgundy – if your principles permit.

ROPER: They don't, sir.

MORE: Well, have some water in it.

ROPER: Just the water, sir.

MORE: My poor boy.

ALICE (*stopping at head of stairs, as one who will be answered.*) Why does Cromwell collect information about you?

MORE: I'm a prominent figure. Someone somewhere's collecting information about Cromwell. Now no more shirking; we must make a start. (*Shepherding* ROPER *up the stairs.*) There's a stuffed swan if you please. (ALICE *and* MARGARET *exit above.*) Will, I'd trust *you* with my life. But not your principles. (*They mount the stairs.*) You see, we speak of being anchored to our principles. But if the weather turns nasty you up with an anchor and let it down where there's less wind, and the fishing's better. And 'look' we say 'I'm anchored!' (*Laughing, inviting* ROPER *to laugh with him.*) 'To my principles!'

Exit above, MORE *and* ROPER. *Enter* COMMON MAN *pulling basket. From it he takes an Inn Sign which he hangs on to the alcove. He inspects it.*

COMMON MAN: 'The Loyal Subject' . . . (*to audience*) a pub (*takes from basket and puts on jacket, cap and napkin*). A publican. (*Places two stools at the table, and mugs and a candle which he lights.*) Oh, he's a deep one that Sir Thomas More. . . . Deep. . . . It takes a lot of education to get a man as deep as that. . . . (*Straight to audience.*) And a deep nature to begin with too. (*Deadpan.*) The likes of me can hardly be *expected* to follow the processes of a man like that. . . . (*Sly.*) Can we? (*Inspects pub.*) Right, ready. (*Goes right.*) Ready, sir!

Enter CROMWELL, *carrying bottle. Goes to alcove.*

CROMWELL: Is this a *good* place for a conspiracy, innkeeper?

PUBLICAN (*woodenly*): You asked for a private room, sir.

CROMWELL (*looking round*): Yes, I want one without too many little dark corners.

PUBLICAN: I don't understand you, sir. Just the four corners as you see.

CROMWELL (*sardonic*): You don't understand me.

PUBLICAN: That's right, sir.

CROMWELL: Do you know who I am?

PUBLICAN (*promptly*): No, sir.

CROMWELL: Don't be too tactful, innkeeper.

PUBLICAN: I don't understand, sir.

CROMWELL: When the likes of you *are* too tactful, the likes of me begin to wonder who's the fool.

PUBLICAN: I just don't understand you, sir.

CROMWELL (*puts back his head and laughs silently*): The master statesman of us all. 'I don't understand.' (*Looks at* PUBLICAN *almost with hatred.*) All right. Get out. (*Throws coin. Exit* PUBLICAN. CROMWELL *goes to exit opposite. Calling.*) Come on. (*Enter* RICH. *He glances at bottle in* CROMWELL'S *hand and remains cautiously by the exit.*) Yes, it may be that I am a little intoxicated. (*Leaves* RICH *standing.*) But not with alcohol, with success! And who has a strong head for success? None of us gets enough of it. Except Kings. And they're born drunk.

RICH: Success? What success?

CROMWELL: Guess.

RICH: Collector of Revenues for York.

CROMWELL (*amused*): You do keep your ear to the ground don't you? No. Better than that.

RICH: High Constable.

CROMWELL: Better than that.

RICH: Better than High Constable?

CROMWELL: Much better. Sir Thomas Paget is – retiring.

RICH: Secretary to the Council!

CROMWELL: 'Tis astonishing, isn't it?

RICH (*hastily*): Oh no – I mean – one sees, it's logical.

CROMWELL: No ceremony, no courtship. Be seated. (RICH *sits.*) As His Majesty would say. (RICH *laughs nervously and involuntarily glances round.*) Yes; see how I trust you.

RICH: Oh, I would never repeat or report a thing like that——

CROMWELL (*pouring wine*): What kind of thing would you repeat or report?

RICH: Well, nothing said in friendship – may I say 'friendship'?

CROMWELL: If you like. D'you believe that – that you would never repeat or report anything etcetera?

RICH: Why yes!

CROMWELL: No, but seriously.

RICH: Yes!

CROMWELL (*puts down bottle. Not sinister, but rather as a kindly teacher with a promising pupil*): Rich; seriously.

RICH (*pauses, then bitterly*): It would depend what I was offered.

CROMWELL: Don't say it just to please me.

RICH: It's true. It would depend what I was offered.

CROMWELL (*patting his arm*): Everyone knows it; not many people can say it.

RICH: There are *some* things one wouldn't do for anything. Surely.

CROMWELL: Mm – that idea's like these lifelines they have on the embankment: comforting, but you don't expect to have to use them. (*Briskly.*) Well, congratulations!

RICH (*suspicious*): On what?

CROMWELL: I think you'd make a good Collector of Revenues for York Diocese.

RICH (*gripping on to himself*): Is it in your gift?

CROMWELL: Effectively.

RICH (*conscious cynicism*): What do I have to do for it?

CROMWELL: Nothing. (*He lectures, pacing pedantically up and down.*) It isn't like that, Rich. There are no rules. With rewards and penalties – so much wickedness purchases so much worldly prospering—— (*He breaks off and stops, suddenly struck.*) Are you sure you're not religious?

RICH: Almost sure.

CROMWELL: Get sure. (*Resumes pacing.*) No, it's not like that, it's much more a matter of convenience, administrative convenience. The normal aim of administration is to keep steady this factor of convenience – and Sir Thomas would agree. Now normally when a man wants to change his woman, you let him if it's convenient and prevent him if it's not – normally indeed it's of so little importance that you leave it to the priests. But the constant factor is this element of convenience.

RICH: Whose convenience? (CROMWELL *stops*.)

CROMWELL: Oh ours. But everybody's too. (*Sets off again*.) However, in the present instance the man who wants to change his woman is our Sovereign Lord, Harry, by the Grace of God, the Eighth of that name. Which is a quaint way of saying that if he wants to change his woman he will. So *that* becomes the constant factor. And our job as administrators is to make it as convenient as we can. I say 'our' job, on the assumption that you'll take this post at York I've offered you?

RICH: Yes . . . yes, yes. (*But he seems gloomy*.)

CROMWELL (*sits. Sharply*): It's a bad sign when people are depressed by their own good fortune.

RICH (*defensive*): I'm not depressed!

CROMWELL: You look depressed.

RICH (*hastily buffooning*): I'm lamenting. I've lost my innocence.

CROMWELL: You lost that some time ago. If you've only just noticed, it can't have been very important to you.

RICH (*much struck*): That's true! Why that's true, it can't!

CROMWELL: We experience a sense of release do we, Master Rich? An unfamiliar freshness in the head, as of open air?

RICH (*takes wine*): Collector of Revenues isn't bad!

CROMWELL: Not bad for a start. (*He watches* RICH *drink*.) Now our present Lord Chancellor – *there's* an innocent man.

RICH (*puts down glass. Indulgently*.) The odd thing is – he *is*.

CROMWELL (*looks at him with dislike*): Yes, I say he is. (*The light tone again*.) The trouble is, his innocence is tangled in this proposition that you can't change your woman without a divorce, and can't have a divorce unless the Pope says so. And although his present Holiness is – judged even by the most liberal standards – a strikingly corrupt old person, yet he still has this word 'Pope' attached to him. And from this quite meaningless circumstance I fear some degree of . . .

RICH (*pleased, waving his cup*): Administrative inconvenience.

CROMWELL (*nodding as to a pupil word perfect*): Just so. (*Dead-*

pan.) This goblet that he gave you, how much was it worth? (RICH *puts down cup, looks down. Quite gently.*) Come along, Rich, he gave you a silver goblet. How much did you get for it?

RICH: Fifty shillings.

CROMWELL: Could you take me to the shop?

RICH: Yes.

CROMWELL: Where did he get it? (*No reply.*) It was a gift from a litigant, a woman, wasn't it?

RICH: Yes.

CROMWELL: Which court? Chancery? (*Restrains* RICH *from filling his glass.*) No, don't get drunk. In which court was this litigant's case?

RICH: Court of Requests.

CROMWELL (*grunts, his face abstracted. Becoming aware of* RICH'S *regard he smiles*): There, that wasn't too painful was it?

RICH (*laughing a little and a little rueful*): No!

CROMWELL (*spreading his hands*): That's all there is. And you'll find it easier next time.

RICH (*looks up briefly, unhappily*): What application do they have, these titbits of information you collect?

CROMWELL: None at all, usually.

RICH (*stubbornly, not looking up*): But sometimes.

CROMWELL: Well, there *are* these men – you know – 'upright', 'steadfast', men who want themselves to be the constant factor in the situation. Which of course they can't be. The situation rolls forward in any case.

RICH (*the same*): So what happens?

CROMWELL (*not liking his tone, coldly*): If they've any sense they get out of its way.

RICH: What if they haven't any sense?

CROMWELL (*the same*): What none at all? Well, then they're only fit for Heaven. But Sir Thomas has plenty of sense; he could be frightened.

RICH (*looks up, his face nasty*): Don't forget he's an innocent, Master Cromwell.

CROMWELL: I think we'll finish there for tonight. (*Rising.*) After all, he *is* the Lord Chancellor. (*Going.*)

RICH: You wouldn't find him easy to frighten! (*Calls after him.*) You've mistaken your man this time! He doesn't know how to be frightened!

CROMWELL (*returning. RICH rises at his approach*): Doesn't know how to be frightened? Why, then he never put his hand in a candle. . . . Did he? (*And seizing RICH by the wrist he holds his hand in the candle flame.*)

RICH (*screeches and darts back, hugging his hand in his armpit, regarding CROMWELL with horror*): You enjoyed that! (CROMWELL'S *downturned face is amazed. Triumphantly.*) You enjoyed it!

CURTAIN

ACT TWO

The scene is as for start of Act One. When the curtain rises the stage is in darkness save for a spot, front stage, in which stands the COMMON MAN. *He carries the book, a place marked by his finger, and wears his spectacles.*

COMMON MAN: The interval started early in the year 1530 and it's now the middle of May 1532. (*Explanatory.*) Two years. During that time a lot of water's flowed under the bridge and among the things that have come floating along on it is ... (*Reads.*) 'The Church of England, that finest flower of our Island genius for compromise; that system, peculiar to these shores, which deflects the torrents of religious passion down the canals of moderation.' That's very well put. (*Returns to book, approvingly.*) 'Typically, this great effect was achieved not by bloodshed but by simple Act of Parliament. Only an unhappy few were found to set themselves against the current of their times, and in so doing to court disaster. For we are dealing with an age less fastidious than our own. Imprisonment without trial, and even examination under torture, were common practice.'

Lights rise to show MORE, *seated, and* ROPER, *standing. Exit* COMMON MAN. ROPER *is dressed in black and wears a cross. He commences to walk up and down, watched by* MORE. *A pause.*

MORE: Must you wear those clothes, Will?

ROPER: Yes, I must.

MORE: Why?

ROPER: The time has come for decent men to declare their allegiance!

MORE: And what allegiance are those designed to express?

ROPER: My allegiance to the Church.

MORE: Well, you *look* like a Spaniard.

ROPER: All credit to Spain then!

MORE: You wouldn't last six months in Spain. You'd have been burned alive in Spain, during your heretic period.

ROPER: I suppose you have the right to remind me of it. (*Points accusingly*). That chain of office that *you* wear is a degradation!

MORE (*glances down at it*): I've told you. If the bishops in Convocation submitted this morning, I'll take it off. . . . It's no degradation. Great men have worn this.

ROPER: When d'you expect to hear from Canterbury?

MORE: About now. The Archbishop promised me an immediate message.

ROPER (*recommences pacing*): I don't see what difference Convocation can make. The Church is already a wing of the Palace is it not? The King is already its 'Supreme Head'! Is he not?

MORE: No.

ROPER (*is startled*): You are denying the Act of Supremacy!

MORE: No, I'm not; the Act states that the King——

ROPER: – is Supreme Head of the Church in England.

MORE: Supreme Head of the Church in England—— (*Underlining the words.*) 'so far as the law of God allows.' How far the law of God does allow it remains a matter of opinion, since the Act doesn't state it.

ROPER: A legal quibble.

MORE: Call it what you like, it's there, thank God.

ROPER: Very well: in your opinion how far does the law of God allow this?

MORE: I'll keep my opinion to myself, Will.

ROPER: Yes? I'll tell you mine——!

MORE: Don't! If your opinion's what I think it is, it's High Treason, Roper!

Enter MARGARET *above, unseen.*

Will, you remember you've a wife now! And may have children!

MARGARET: Why must he remember that?

ROPER: To keep myself 'discreet'.

MARGARET (*smiling*): Then I'd rather you forgot it.

MORE (*unsmiling*): You are either idiots, or children.
Enter CHAPUYS, *above*.

CHAPUYS: Or saints, my lord! (*Very sonorous.*)

MARGARET: Oh, Father, Signor Chapuys has come to see you.

MORE (*rising*): Your Excellency.

CHAPUYS (*strikes pose with* MARGARET *and* ROPER): Or saints, my lord; or saints.

MORE (*grins maliciously at* ROPER): That's it of course – saints! Roper – turn your head a bit – yes, I think I do detect, a faint radiance. (*Reproachful.*) You should have told us, Will.

CHAPUYS: Come come, my lord; you too at this time are not free from some suspicion of saintliness.

MORE (*quietly*): I don't like the sound of that, Your Excellency. What do you require of *me*? What, Your Excellency?

CHAPUYS (*awkward beneath his sudden keen regard*): May I not come simply, to pay my respects to the English Socrates – as I see your angelic friend Erasmus calls you.

MORE (*wrinkles nose*): Yes, I'll think of something presently to call Erasmus. (*Checks.*) Socrates! I've no taste for hemlock, Your Excellency, if that's what you require.

CHAPUYS (*display of horror*): Heaven forbid!

MORE (*dryly*): Amen.

CHAPUYS (*spreads hands*): Must I require anything? (*Sonorous.*) After all, we are brothers in Christ, you and I!

MORE: A characteristic we share with the rest of humanity. You live in Cheapside, Signor? To make contact with a brother in Christ you have only to open your window and empty a chamberpot. There was no need to come to Chelsea. (CHAPUYS *titters nervously. Coldly.*) William. The Imperial Ambassador is here on business. Would you mind?

ROPER *and* MARGARET *going.*

CHAPUYS (*rising, unreal protestations*): Oh no! I protest!

MORE: He is clearly here on business.

CHAPUYS (*the same*): No; but really, I protest! (*It is no more than token: when* ROPER *and* MARGARET *reach head of stairs he calls:*) Dominus vobiscum filii mei!

ROPER (*pompous*): Et cum spiritu tuo, excellencis!

  Exit ROPER *and* MARGARET.

CHAPUYS (*approaching* MORE, *thrillingly*): And how much longer shall we hear that holy language in these shores?

MORE (*alert, poker-faced*): 'Tisn't 'holy', Your Excellency; just old.

  CHAPUYS *sits with the air of one coming to brass tacks*

CHAPUYS: My Lord, I cannot believe you will allow yourself to be associated with the recent actions of King Henry! In respect of Queen Catherine.

MORE: Subjects are associated with the actions of Kings willy-nilly.

CHAPUYS: The Lord Chancellor is not an ordinary subject. He bears responsibility (*he lets the word sink in;* MORE *shifts*) for what is done.

MORE (*agitation begins to show through*): Have you considered that what has been done badly, might have been done worse, with a different Chancellor.

CHAPUYS (*mounting confidence, as* MORE'S *attention is caught*): Believe me, Sir Thomas, your influence in these policies has been much searched for, and where it has been found it has been praised – *but* . . . There comes a point, does there not? . . .

MORE: Yes. (*Agitated.*) There does come such a point.

CHAPUYS: When the sufferings of one unfortunate lady swell to an open attack on the religion of an entire country that point has been passed. Beyond that point, Sir Thomas, one is not merely 'compromised', one is in truth corrupted.

MORE (*stares at him*): What do you want?

CHAPUYS: Rumour has it that if the Church in Convocation has submitted to the King, you will resign.

MORE (*looks down and regains composure*): I see. (*Suave.*) Supposing rumour to be right. Would you approve of that?

CHAPUYS: Approve, applaud, admire.

MORE (*still looking down*): Why?

CHAPUYS: Because it would show one man – and that man known to be temperate – unable to go further with this wickedness.

MORE (*the same*): And that man known to be Chancellor of England too.

CHAPUYS: Believe me, my lord, such a signal would be seen——

MORE (*the same*): 'Signal'?

CHAPUYS: Yes, my lord; it would be seen and understood.

MORE (*the same, and now positively silky*): By whom?

CHAPUYS: By half of your fellow countrymen! (*Now* MORE *looks up sharply*). Sir Thomas, I have just returned from Yorkshire and Northumberland, where I have made a tour.

MORE (*softly*): Have you indeed?

CHAPUYS: Things are very different there, my lord. There they are ready.

MORE: For what?

CHAPUYS: Resistance!

Enter ROPER, *above, excited.*

ROPER: Sir Thomas——! (MORE *looks up angrily*.) Excuse me, sir—— (*Indicates off.*) His Grace the Duke of Norfolk—— (MORE *and* CHAPUYS *rise.* ROPER *excitedly descends.*) It's all over, sir, they've——

Enter NORFOLK *above,* ALICE *and* MARGARET, *below.*

NORFOLK: One moment, Roper, I'll do this! Thomas—— (*Sees* CHAPUYS.) Oh. (*He stares at* CHAPUYS, *hostile.*)

CHAPUYS: I was on the point of leaving, Your Grace. Just a personal call. I have been trying . . . er to borrow a book – but without success – you're sure you have no copy, my

lord? Then I'll leave you. (*Bowing.*) Gentlemen, ladies.
(*Going, up stairs. Stops unseen as* ROPER *speaks.*)

ROPER: Sir Thomas——

NORFOLK: I'll do it, Roper! Convocation's knuckled under,
Thomas. They're to pay a fine of a hundred thousand pounds.
And . . . we've severed the connection with Rome.

MORE (*smiling bitterly*): 'The connection with Rome' is nice.
(*Bitter.*) 'The connection with Rome.' Did *anyone* resist?

NORFOLK: Bishop Fisher.

MORE: Lovely man. (NORFOLK *shrugs.*)

ROPER (*looking at* MORE): Your Grace, this is quite certain is it?

NORFOLK: Yes. (MORE *puts his hand to his chain.* CHAPUYS
exit. All turn.) Funny company, Thomas?

MORE: It's quite unintentional. He doesn't mean to be funny.
(*Fumbles with chain.*) Help me with this.

NORFOLK: Not I.

ROPER (*takes a step forward. Then, subdued*): Shall I, sir?

MORE: No thank you, Will. Alice?

ALICE: Hell's fire – God's blood and body *no*! Sun and moon,
Master More, you're taken for a wise man! Is this wisdom –
to betray your ability, abandon practice, forget your station
and your duty to your kin and behave like a printed book!

MORE (*listens gravely: then*): Margaret, will you?

MARGARET: If you want.

MORE: There's my clever girl. (*She takes it from his neck.*)

NORFOLK: Well, Thomas, why? Make me understand –
because I'll tell you now, from where I stand, this looks like
cowardice!

MORE (*excited and angry*): All right I will – this isn't 'Reforma-
tion'; this is war against the Church! . . . (*Indignant.*) Our
King, Norfolk, has declared war on the Pope – because the
Pope will not declare that our Queen is not his wife.

NORFOLK: And is she?

MORE (*cunning*): I'll answer that question for one person only,
the King. Aye, and that in private too.

NORFOLK (*contemptuous*): Man, you're cautious.

MORE: Yes, cautious. I'm not one of your hawks.

NORFOLK (*walks away and turns*): All right – we're at war with the Pope! The Pope's a Prince, isn't he?

MORE: He is.

NORFOLK: And a bad one?

MORE: Bad enough. But the theory is that he's also the Vicar of God, the descendant of St Peter, our only link with Christ.

NORFOLK (*sneer*): A tenuous link.

MORE: Oh, tenuous indeed.

NORFOLK (*to the others*): Does this make sense? (*No reply; they look at* MORE.) You'll forfeit all you've got – which includes the respect of your country – for a theory?

MORE (*hotly*): The Apostolic Succession of the Pope is—— (*Stops: interested.*) . . . Why, it's a theory yes; you can't see it; can't touch it; it's a theory. (*To* NORFOLK, *very rapid but calm.*) But what matters to me is not whether it's true or not but that I believe it to be true, or rather not that I *believe* it, but that *I* believe it . . . I trust I make myself obscure?

NORFOLK: Perfectly.

MORE: That's good. Obscurity's what I have need of now.

NORFOLK: Man, you're sick. This isn't Spain you know.

MORE (*looks at him: takes him aside: lowered voice*): Have I your word, that what we say here is between us and has no existence beyond these walls?

NORFOLK (*impatient*): Very well.

MORE (*almost whispering*): And if the King should command you to repeat what I have said?

NORFOLK: I should keep my word to you!

MORE: Then what has become of your oath of obedience to the King?

NORFOLK (*indignant*): You lay traps for me!

MORE (*now grown calm*): No, I show you the times.

NORFOLK: Why do you insult me with these lawyer's tricks?

MORE: Because I am afraid.

NORFOLK: And here's your answer. The King accepts your resignation very sadly; he is mindful of your goodness and past loyalty and in any matter concerning your honour and welfare he will be your good lord. So much for your fear.

MORE (*flatly*): You will convey my humble gratitude.

NORFOLK: I will. Good day, Alice (*Going.*) I'd rather deal with you than your husband.

MORE (*complete change of tone; briskly professional*): Oh, Howard! (*Goes to him.*) Signor Chapuys tells me he's just made a 'tour' of the North Country. He thinks we shall have trouble there. So do I.

NORFOLK (*stolid*): Yes? What kind of trouble?

MORE: The Church – the old Church, not the new Church – is, very strong up there. I'm serious, Howard, keep an eye on the Border, this next year; and bear in mind the Old Alliance.

NORFOLK (*looks at him*): We will. We do.... As for the Dago, Thomas, it'll perhaps relieve your mind to know that one of Secretary Cromwell's agents made the tour with him.

MORE: Oh. (*Flash of jealousy.*) Of course if Master Cromwell has matters in hand——

NORFOLK: – He has.

MORE: Yes, I can imagine.

NORFOLK: But thanks for the information. (*Going.*) It's good to know you still have . . . some vestige of patriotism.

MORE (*anger*): That's a remarkably stupid observation, Norfolk!

    Exit NORFOLK.

ALICE: So there's an end of you. What will you do now – sit by the fire and make goslings in the ash?

MORE: Not at all, Alice, I expect I'll write a bit. (*He woos them with unhappy cheerfulness.*) I'll write, I'll read, I'll think. I think I'll learn to fish! I'll play with my grandchildren – when son Roper's done his duty. (*Eager.*) Alice, shall I teach you to read?

ALICE: No, by God!

MORE: . . . Son Roper, *you're* pleased with me I hope?

ROPER (*goes to him: moved*): Sir, you've made a noble gesture.

MORE (*blankly*): A gesture? (*Eager.*) It wasn't possible to continue, Will. I was not *able* to continue. I would have if I could! I make no gesture! (*Apprehensive, looks after* NORFOLK.) My God, I hope it's understood I make no gesture! (*Turns back to them.*) – Alice, you don't think I would do this to you for a gesture! *That's* a gesture! (*Thumbs his nose.*) *That's* a gesture! (*Jerks up two fingers.*) I'm no street acrobat to make gestures! I'm practical!

ROPER: You belittle yourself, sir, this was not practical; (*resonant*) this was moral!

MORE: Oh now I understand you, Will. Morality's *not* practical. Morality's a gesture. A complicated gesture learned from books – that's what you say, Alice, isn't it? . . . And you, Meg?

MARGARET: It *is*, for most of us, Father.

MORE: Oh no, if you're going to plead humility——! Oh, you're cruel. I have a cruel family.

ALICE: Yes, you can fit the cap on anyone you want, I know that well enough. If there's cruelty in this house, I know where to look for it.

MARGARET: No, Mother——!

ALICE: Oh, you'd walk on the bottom of the sea and think yourself a crab if he suggested it! (*To* ROPER.) And you! You'd dance him to the Tower—— You'd dance him to the block! Like David with a harp! Scattering hymn-books in his path! (*To* MORE.) Poor silly man, d'you think they'll *leave* you here to learn to fish?

MORE (*straight at her*): If we govern our tongues they will! . . . Look, I have a word to say about that. I have made no statement. I've resigned, that's *all*. On the King's Supremacy, the King's divorce which he'll now grant himself, the marriage he'll then make – have you heard me make a statement?

ALICE: No – and if I'm to lose my rank and fall to housekeeping I want to know the reason; so make a statement now.

MORE: No – (ALICE *exhibits indignation*) – Alice, it's a point of law! Accept it from me, Alice, that in silence is my safety under the law, but my silence must be absolute, it must extend to you.

ALICE: In short you don't trust us!

MORE (*impatient*): Look – (*advances on her*) I'm the Lord Chief Justice, I'm Cromwell, I'm the King's Head Jailer – and I take your hand (*does so*) and I clamp it on the Bible, on the Blessed Cross (*clamps her hand on his closed fist*) and I say: 'Woman, has your husband made a statement on these matters?' Now – on peril of your soul remember – what's your answer?

ALICE: No.

MORE: And so it must remain. (*He looks round at their grave faces.*) Oh, it's only a life-line, we shan't have to use it but it's comforting to have. No, no, when they find I'm silent they'll ask nothing better than to leave me silent; you'll see.

    Enter STEWARD.

STEWARD: Sir, the household's in the kitchen. They want to know what's happened.

MORE: Oh. Yes. We must speak to them. Alice, they'll mostly have to go, my dear. (*To* STEWARD.) But not before we've found them places.

ALICE: We can't find places for them all!

MORE: Yes, we can; yes, we can. Tell them so.

ALICE: God's death it comes on us quickly…

    Exit ALICE, MARGARET *and* ROPER.

MORE: What about you, Matthew? It'll be a smaller household now, and for you I'm afraid, a smaller wage. Will you stay?

STEWARD: Don't see how I could then, sir.

MORE: You're a single man.

STEWARD (*awkward*): Well, yes, sir, but I mean I've got my own——

MORE (*quickly*): Quite right, why should you? . . . I shall miss you, Matthew.

STEWARD (*man to man jocosity*): No-o-o. You never had much time for *me*, sir. You see through *me*, sir, I know that. (*He almost winks.*)

MORE (*gently insists*): I shall miss you, Matthew; I shall miss you.

Exit MORE. STEWARD *snatches off hat and hurls it to the floor.*

STEWARD: Now, damn me isn't that them all over! (*He broods, face downturned.*) Miss——? . . . He—— . . . Miss——? . . . *Miss* me? . . . What's *in* me for *him* to miss. . . ? (*Suddenly he cries out like one who sees a danger at his very feet.*) Wo-AH! (*Chuckling.*) We-e-eyup! (*To audience.*) I nearly fell for it. (*Walks away.*) 'Matthew, will you kindly take a cut in your wages?' 'No, Sir Thomas, I will not.' That's it and (*fiercely*) that's all of it! (*Falls to thought again. Resentfully.*) All right so he's down on his luck! I'm sorry. I don't mind saying that: I'm sorry! Bad luck! If I'd any good luck to spare he could have some. I wish we could *all* have good luck, *all* the time! I wish we had wings! I wish rainwater was beer! But it isn't! . . . And what with not having wings but walking – on two flat feet; and good luck and bad luck being just exactly even stevens; and rain being water – don't you complicate the job by putting things in me for me to miss! (*He takes off* STEWARD'S *coat, picks up his hat: draws the curtain to alcove. Chuckling.*) I did you know. I nearly fell for it.

Exit COMMON MAN. NORFOLK *and* CROMWELL *enter to alcove.*

NORFOLK: But he makes no noise, Mr Secretary; he's silent, why not leave him silent?

CROMWELL (*patiently*): Not being a man of letters, Your Grace, you perhaps don't realise the extent of his reputation. This 'silence' of his is bellowing up and down Europe! Now may I recapitulate: He reported the Ambassador's conversation to you, informed on the Ambassador's tour of the North-country, warned against a possible rebellion there.

NORFOLK: He did!

CROMWELL: We may say then, that he showed himself hostile to the hopes of Spain.

NORFOLK: That's what I *say*!

CROMWELL (*patiently*): Bear with me, Your Grace. Now if he opposes Spain, he supports us. Well, surely that follows? (*Sarcastically*.) Or do you see some third alternative?

NORFOLK: No no, that's the line-up all right. And I may say Thomas More——

CROMWELL: Thomas More will line up on the right side.

NORFOLK: Yes! Crank he may be, traitor he is not.

CROMWELL (*spreading his hands*): And with a little pressure, he can be got to say so. And that's all we need – a brief declaration of his loyalty to the present administration.

NORFOLK: I still say let sleeping dogs lie. (I leave More alone)

CROMWELL (*heavily*): The King does not agree with you.

NORFOLK (*glances at him; flickers, but then rallies*): What kind of 'pressure' d'you think you can bring to bear?

CROMWELL: I have evidence that Sir Thomas, during the period of his judicature, accepted bribes.

NORFOLK (*incredulous*): What! Goddammit he was the only judge since Cato who *didn't* accept bribes! When was there last a Chancellor whose possessions after three years in office totalled one hundred pounds and a gold chain.

CROMWELL (*rings hand-bell and calls*): Richard! It is, as you imply, common practice, but a practice may be common and remain an offence; this offence could send a man to the Tower.

NORFOLK (*contemptuous*): I don't believe it.

  Enter RICH *and* A WOMAN. *He motions her to remain, and*

approaches the table, where CROMWELL *indicates a seat. He has acquired self-importance.*

CROMWELL: Ah, Richard. You know His Grace of course.

RICH (*respectful affability*): Indeed yes, we're *old* friends.

NORFOLK (*savage snub*): Used to look after my books or something, didn't you?

CROMWELL (*clicks his fingers at* WOMAN): Come here. This woman's name is Catherine Anger; she comes from Lincoln. And she put a case in the Court of Requests in—— (*Consults paper.*)

WOMAN: A property case, it was.

CROMWELL: Be quiet. A property case in the Court of Requests in April 1526.

WOMAN: And got a wicked false judgement!

CROMWELL: And got an impeccably correct judgement from our friend Sir Thomas.

WOMAN: No, sir, it was not!

CROMWELL: We're not concerned with the judgement but the gift you gave the judge. Tell this gentleman about that. The judgement for what it's worth was the right one.

WOMAN: No, sir! (CROMWELL *looks at her: she hastily addresses* NORFOLK.) I sent him a cup, sir; an Italian Silver cup I bought in Lincoln for a hundred shillings.

NORFOLK: Did Sir Thomas accept this cup?

WOMAN: I sent it.

CROMWELL: He did accept it, we can corroborate that. You can go. (*She opens her mouth.*) Go! (*Exit* WOMAN.

NORFOLK (*scornful*): Is that your witness?

CROMWELL: No; by an odd coincidence this cup later came into the hands of Master Rich here.

NORFOLK: How?

RICH: He gave it to me.

NORFOLK (*brutal*): Can you corroborate that?

CROMWELL: I have a fellow outside who can; he was More's

steward at that time. Shall I call him?

NORFOLK: Don't bother, I know him. When did Thomas give you this thing?

RICH: I don't exactly remember.

NORFOLK: Well, make an effort. Wait! I can tell you! I can tell you – it was that Spring – it was that night we were there together. You had a cup with you when we left; was that it?

RICH *looks to* CROMWELL *for guidance but gets none.*

RICH: It may have been.

NORFOLK: Did he often give you cups?

RICH: I don't suppose so, Your Grace.

NORFOLK: That was it then. (*New realisation.*) And it was April! The April of 26. The very month that cow first put her case before him! (*Triumphant.*) In other words the moment he knew it was a bribe, he got rid of it.

CROMWELL (*nodding judicially*): The facts will bear that interpretation I suppose.

NORFOLK: Oh, this is a horse that won't run, Master Secretary.

CROMWELL: Just a trial canter, Your Grace. We'll find something better.

NORFOLK (*between bullying and plea*): Look here, Cromwell, I want no part of this. (wants more left alone)

CROMWELL: You have no choice.

NORFOLK: What's that you say?

CROMWELL: The King particularly wishes you to be active in the matter.

NORFOLK (*winded*): He has not told me that.

CROMWELL (*politely*): Indeed? He told me.

NORFOLK: But *why*?

CROMWELL: We feel that, since you are known to have been a friend of More's, your participation will show that there is nothing in the nature of a 'persecution', but only the strict processes of law. As indeed you've just demonstrated. I'll tell the King of your loyalty to your friend. If you like, I'll tell him that you 'want no part of it', too.

NORFOLK (*furious*): Are you threatening me, Cromwell?

CROMWELL: My *dear* Norfolk. . . . This isn't Spain.

>   NORFOLK *stares, turns abruptly and exit.* CROMWELL *turns a look of glacial coldness upon* RICH.

RICH: I'm sorry, secretary, I'd forgotten he was there that night.

CROMWELL (*scrutinises him dispassionately, then*): You must try to remember these things.

RICH: Secretary, I'm sincerely——!

CROMWELL (*dismisses the topic with a wave and turns to look after* NORFOLK): Not such a fool as he looks, the Duke.

RICH (*Civil Service simper*): That would hardly be possible, Secretary.

CROMWELL (*straightening papers, briskly*): Sir Thomas is going to be a slippery fish, Richard; we need a net with a finer mesh.

RICH: Yes, Secretary?

CROMWELL: We'll weave one for him shall we, you and I?

RICH (*uncertain*): I'm only anxious to do what is correct, Secretary.

CROMWELL (*smiling at him*): Yes, Richard, I know. (*Straight-faced.*) You're absolutely right, it must be done by law. It's just a matter of finding the right law. Or making one. Bring my papers, will you?

>   *Exit* CROMWELL. *Enter* STEWARD.

STEWARD: Could we have a word now, sir?

RICH: We don't require you after all, Matthew.

STEWARD: No, sir, but about . . .

RICH: Oh yes. . . . Well, I begin to need a steward, certainly; my household is expanding. . . . (*Sharply.*) But as I remember, Matthew, your attitude to me was sometimes – disrespectful! (*The last word is shrill.*)

STEWARD (*with humble dignity*): Oh. Oh, I must contradict you there, sir; that's your imagination. In those days, sir, you still had your way to make. And a gentleman in that position often imagines these things. Then when he's risen to his proper level, sir, he stops thinking about it. (*As one offering tangible proof.*) Well – I don't think you find people 'disrespectful' nowadays, do you, sir?

RICH: There may be something in that. Bring my papers. (*Going, turns at exit and anxiously scans* STEWARD'*s face for signs of impudence.*) I'll permit no breath of insolence!

STEWARD (*the very idea is shocking*): I should hope not, sir. (*Exit* RICH.) Oh, I can manage this one! He's just my size! (*Lighting changes so that the set looks drab and chilly.*) Sir Thomas More's again gone down a bit.

   Exit COMMON MAN.

Enter, side, CHAPUYS *and* ATTENDANT, *cloaked. Above,* ALICE, *wearing big coarse apron over her dress.*

ALICE: My husband is coming down, Your Excellency.

CHAPUYS: Thank you, madam.

ALICE: And I beg you to be gone before he does!

CHAPUYS (*patiently*): Madam, I have a Royal Commission to perform.

ALICE: Aye. You said so. (*Exit* ALICE.)

CHAPUYS: For sheer barbarity, commend me to a good-hearted Englishwoman of a certain class. . . . (*Wraps cloak about him.*)

ATTENDANT: It's very cold, Excellency.

CHAPUYS: I remember when these rooms were warm enough.

ATTENDANT (*looking about*): 'Thus it is to incur the enmity of a Prince.'

CHAPUYS: – A heretic Prince. (*Looking about.*) Yes, Sir Thomas is a good man.

ATTENDANT: Yes, Excellency, I like Sir Thomas very much.

CHAPUYS: Carefully, carefully.

ATTENDANT: It's uncomfortable dealing with him, isn't it?

CHAPUYS: Goodness presents its own difficulties. Attend and learn now.

ATTENDANT: Excellency?

CHAPUYS: Well?

ATTENDANT: Excellency, is he really *for* us?

CHAPUYS (*testy*): He's opposed to Cromwell. He's shown that, I think?

ATTENDANT: Yes, Excellency, but——

CHAPUYS: If he's opposed to Cromwell, he's for us. There's no third alternative.

ATTENDANT: I suppose not, Excellency.

CHAPUYS: I wish your mother had chosen some other career for you; you've no political sense whatever. Sh!

Enter MORE. *His clothes match the atmosphere of the room and he moves rather more deliberately than before.*

MORE (*descending*): Is this another 'personal' visit, Chapuys, or is it official?

CHAPUYS: It falls between the two, Sir Thomas.

MORE (*reaching the bottom of stairs*): Official then.

CHAPUYS: No, I have a personal letter for you.

MORE: From whom?

CHAPUYS: From King Charles! (MORE *puts hands behind back.*) You will take it?

MORE: I will not lay a finger on it.

CHAPUYS: It is in no way an affair of State. It expresses my master's admiration for the stand which you and Bishop Fisher of Rochester have taken over the so-called divorce of Queen Catherine.

MORE: I have taken no stand!

CHAPUYS: But your views, Sir Thomas, are well known——

MORE: My views are much guessed at. (*Irritably*.) Oh come, sir, could you undertake to convince (*grimly*) King Harry that this letter is 'in no way an affair of State?'

CHAPUYS: My dear Sir Thomas, I have taken extreme precautions. I came here very much incognito. (*Self-indulgent chuckle.*) Very nearly in disguise.

MORE: You misunderstand me. It is not a matter of your precautions but my duty; which would be to take this letter immediately to the King.

CHAPUYS (*flabbergasted*): But, Sir Thomas, your views——

MORE: – Are well known you say. It seems my loyalty is less so.
> *Enter* MARGARET *bearing before her a huge bundle of bracken.*

MARGARET: Look, Father! (*Dumps it.*) Will's getting more.

MORE: Oh, well done! (*Not whimsy; they're cold and their interest in fuel is serious.*) Is it dry? (*Feels it expertly.*) Oh it *is.* (*Sees* CHAPUYS *staring; laughs.*) It's bracken, Your Excellency. We burn it. (*Enter* ALICE.) Alice, look at this. (*The bracken.*)

ALICE (*eyeing* CHAPUYS): Aye.

MORE (*crossing to* CHAPUYS): May I——? (*Takes letter to* ALICE *and* MARGARET.) This is a letter from King Charles; I want you to see it's not been opened. I have declined it. You see the seal has not been broken? (*Returning it to* CHAPUYS.) I wish I could ask you to stay, Your Excellency – the bracken fire is a luxury.

CHAPUYS (*cold smile*): One I must forego. (*Aside to* ATTENDANT.) Come. (*Crosses to exit, pauses.*) May I say I am sure my master's admiration will not be diminished. (*Bows.*)

MORE: I am gratified. (*Bows, women curtsey.*)

CHAPUYS (*aside to* ATTENDANT): The man's utterly unreliable!
> *Exit* CHAPUYS *and* ATTENDANT.

ALICE (*after a little silence kicks the bracken*): 'Luxury!' (*She sits wearily on the bundle.*)

MORE: Well, it's a luxury while it lasts. . . . There's not much sport in it for you, is there? . . . (*She neither answers nor looks at him from the depths of her fatigue. After a moment's hesitation he braces himself.*) Alice, the money from the Bishops. I wish – oh heaven how I wish I could take it! But I can't.

ALICE (*as one who has ceased to expect anything*): I didn't think you would.

MORE (*reproachful*): Alice, there *are* reasons.

ALICE: We couldn't come so deep into your confidence as to *know* these reasons why a man in poverty can't take four thousand pounds?

MORE (*gently but very firm*): Alice, this isn't poverty.

ALICE: D'you know what we shall eat tonight?

MORE (*trying for a smile*): Yes, parsnips.

ALICE: Yes, parsnips and stinking mutton! (*Straight at him.*) For a knight's lady!

MORE (*pleading*): But at the worst, we could be beggars, and still keep company, and be merry together!

ALICE (*bitterly*): Merry!

MORE (*sternly*): Aye, merry!

MARGARET (*her arm about her mother's waist*): I think you should take that money.

MORE: Oh, don't you see? (*Sits by them.*) If I'm paid by the Church for my writings——

ALICE: – This had nothing to do with your writings! This was charity pure and simple! Collected from the clergy high and low!

MORE: It would *appear* as payment.

ALICE: You're not a man who deals in appearances!

MORE (*fervent*): Oh, am I not though. . . . (*Calmly.*) If the King takes this matter any further, with me or with the Church, it will be very bad, if I even appear to have been in the pay of the Church.

ALICE (*sharply*): Bad?

MORE: If you will have it, dangerous. (*He gets up.*)

MARGARET: But you don't write against the King.

MORE: I write! And that's enough in times like these!

ALICE: You said there *was* no danger!

MORE: I don't think there is! And I don't want there to be!

    Enter ROPER *carrying sickle.*

ROPER (*steadily*): There's a gentleman here from Hampton Court. You are to go before Secretary Cromwell. To answer certain charges. (ALICE *and* MARGARET, *appalled, turn to* MORE.)

MORE (*after a silence, rubs his nose*): Well, that's all right. We expected that. (*Not very convincing.*) When?

ROPER: Now. (ALICE *exhibits distress.*)

MORE: That means nothing, Alice; that's just technique. . . . Well, I suppose 'now' means now.

   Lighting change commences, darkness gathering on the others, leaving MORE *isolated in the light, out of which he answers them in the shadows.*

MARGARET: Can I come with you?

MORE: Why? No. I'll be back for dinner. I'll bring Cromwell to dinner, shall I? It'd serve him right.

MARGARET: Oh, Father, don't be witty!

MORE: Why not? Wit's what's in question.

ROPER (*quietly*): While we are witty, the Devil may enter us unawares.

MORE: He's not the Devil, son Roper, he's a lawyer! And my case is watertight!

ALICE: They say he's a very nimble lawyer.

MORE: What, Cromwell? Pooh, he's a pragmatist – and that's the only resemblance he has to the Devil, son Roper; a pragmatist, the merest plumber.

   Sc 4   *Exit* ALICE, MARGARET, ROPER, *in darkness.*

   Sc 4

   Lights come up. Enter CROMWELL, *bustling, carrying file of papers.*

CROMWELL: I'm sorry to invite you here at such short notice, Sir Thomas; good of you to come. (*Draws back curtain from alcove, revealing* RICH *seated at table, with writing materials.*) Will you take a seat? I think you know Master Rich?

MORE: Indeed yes, we're old friends. That's a nice gown you have, Richard.

CROMWELL: Master Rich will make a record of our conversation.

MORE: Good of you to tell me, Master Secretary.

CROMWELL (*laughs appreciatively. Then*): Believe me, Sir Thomas – no, that's asking too much – but let me tell you all the same, you have no more sincere admirer than myself.

(RICH *begins to scribble*.) Not yet, Rich, not yet. (*Invites* MORE *to join him in laughing at* RICH.)

MORE: If I might hear the charges?

CROMWELL: Charges?

MORE: I understand there are certain charges.

CROMWELL: Some ambiguities of behaviour I should like to clarify – hardly 'charges'.

MORE: Make a note of that will you, Master Rich? There are no charges.

CROMWELL (*laughing and shaking head*): Sir Thomas, Sir Thomas. . . . You know it amazes me that you, who were once so effective *in* the world, and are now so *much* retired from it, should be opposing yourself to the whole movement of the times? (*He ends on a note of interrogation.*)

MORE (*nods*): It amazes me too.

CROMWELL (*picks up and drops paper. Sadly*): The King is not pleased with you.

MORE: I am grieved.

CROMWELL: Yet do you know that even now, if you could bring yourself to agree with the Universities, the Bishops, and the Parliament of this realm, there is no honour which the King would be likely to deny you?

MORE (*stonily*): I am well acquainted with His Graces' generosity.

CROMWELL (*coldly*): Very well. (*Consults paper.*) You have heard of the so-called 'Holy Maid of Kent' – who was executed for prophesying against the King?

MORE: Yes; I knew the poor woman.

CROMWELL (*quick*): You sympathise with her?

MORE: She was ignorant and misguided; she was a bit mad I think. And she has paid for her folly. Naturally I sympathise with her.

CROMWELL (*grunts*): You admit meeting her. You met her – and yet you did not warn His Majesty of her treason. How was that?

MORE: She spoke no treason. Our conversation was not political.

CROMWELL: My dear More, the woman was notorious! Do you expect me to believe that?

MORE: Happily there were witnesses.

CROMWELL: You wrote a letter to her?

MORE: Yes, I wrote advising her to abstain from meddling with the affairs of Princes and the State. I have a copy of this letter – also witnessed.

CROMWELL: You have been cautious.

MORE: I like to keep my affairs regular.

CROMWELL: Sir Thomas, there is a more serious charge——

MORE: Charge?

CROMWELL: For want of a better word. In the May of 1526 the King published a book, (*he permits himself a little smile*) a theological work. It was called *A Defence of the Seven Sacraments*.

MORE: Yes. (*Bitterly.*) For which he was named 'Defender of the Faith', by His Holiness the Pope.

CROMWELL: – By the Bishop of Rome. Or do you insist on 'Pope'?

MORE: No, 'Bishop of Rome' if you like. It doesn't alter his authority.

CROMWELL: Thank you, you come to the point very readily; what *is* that authority? As regards the Church in other parts of Europe; (*approaching*) for example, the Church in England. What exactly *is* the Bishop of Rome's authority?

MORE: You will find it very ably set out and defended, Master Secretary, in the King's book.

CROMWELL: The book published under the King's name would be more accurate. You wrote that book.

MORE: – I wrote no part of it.

CROMWELL: – I do not mean you actually held the pen.

MORE: – I merely answered to the best of my ability certain

questions on canon law which His Majesty put to me. As I was bound to do.

CROMWELL: – Do you deny that you *instigated* it?

MORE: – It was from first to last the King's own project. This is trivial, Master Cromwell.

CROMWELL: I should not think so if I were in your place.

MORE: Only two people know the truth of the matter. Myself and the King. And, whatever he may have said to you, he will not give evidence to support this accusation.

CROMWELL: Why not?

MORE: Because evidence is given on oath, and he will not perjure himself. If you don't know that, you don't yet know him. (CROMWELL *looks at him viciously*.)

CROMWELL (*goes apart, formally*): Sir Thomas More, is there anything you wish to say to me concerning the King's marriage with Queen Anne?

MORE (*very still*): I understood I was not to be asked that again.

CROMWELL: Evidently you understood wrongly. These charges——

MORE (*anger breaking through*): They are terrors for children, Mr Secretary, not for me!

CROMWELL: Then know that the King commands me to charge you in his name with great ingratitude! And to tell you that there never was nor never could be so villainous a servant nor so traitorous a subject as yourself!

MORE: So I am brought here at last.

CROMWELL: Brought? You brought yourself to where you stand now.

MORE: Yes. Still, in another sense I was brought.

CROMWELL (*indifferent*): Oh yes. (*Official.*) You may go home now. For the present. (*Exit* MORE.) I don't like him so well as I did. There's a man who raises the gale and won't come out of harbour.

Scene change commences here, i.e., rear of stage becoming water patterned.

RICH (*covert jeer*): Do you still think you can frighten him?

CROMWELL: No, he's misusing his intelligence.

RICH: What will you do now, then?

CROMWELL (*as to an importunate child*): Oh, be quiet, Rich. . . . We'll do whatever's necessary. The King's a man of conscience and he wants either Sir Thomas More to bless his marriage or Sir Thomas More destroyed. Either will do.

RICH (*shakily*): They seem odd alternatives, Secretary.

CROMWELL: Do they? That's because you're not a man of conscience. If the King destroys a man, that's proof to the King that it must have been a bad man, the kind of man a man of conscience *ought* to destroy – and of course a bad man's blessing's not worth having. So either will do.

RICH (*subdued*): I see.

CROMWELL: Oh, there's no going back, Rich. I find we've made ourselves the keepers of this conscience. And it's ravenous.

Exit CROMWELL *and* RICH.

Enter MORE.

MORE (*calling*): Boat! . . . Boat! . . . (*To himself.*) Oh, come along, it's not as bad as that. . . . (*Calls.*) Boat!

Enter NORFOLK. *He stops.*

(*Pleased.*) Howard! . . . I can't get home. They won't bring me a boat.

NORFOLK: Do you blame them?

MORE: Is it as bad as that?

NORFOLK: It's every bit as bad as that!

MORE (*gravely*): Then it's good of you to be seen with me.

NORFOLK (*looking back, off*): I followed you.

MORE (*surprised*): Were *you* followed?

NORFOLK: Probably. (*Facing him.*) So listen to what I have to say: You're behaving like a fool. You're behaving like a crank. You're not behaving like a gentleman—— All right, that means nothing to you; but what about your friends?

MORE: What about them?

NORFOLK: Goddammit, you're dangerous to know!

MORE: Then don't know me.

NORFOLK: There's something further. . . You must have realised by now there's a . . . policy, with regard to you. (MORE *nods*.) The King is using me in it.

MORE: That's clever. That's Cromwell. . . . You're between the upper and the nether millstones then.

NORFOLK: I am!

MORE: Howard, you must cease to know me.

NORFOLK: I do know you! I wish I didn't but I do!

MORE: I mean as a friend.

NORFOLK: You *are* my friend!

MORE: I can't relieve you of your obedience to the King, Howard. You must relieve yourself of our friendship. No one's safe now, and you have a son.

NORFOLK: You might as well advise a man to change the colour of his hair! I'm fond of you, and there it is! You're fond of me, and there it is!

MORE: What's to be done then?

NORFOLK (*with deep appeal*): Give in.

MORE (*gently*): I can't give in, Howard – (*smile*) you might as well advise a man to change the colour of his eyes. I can't. Our friendship's more mutable than *that*. *can be changed.*

NORFOLK: Oh, that's immutable is it? The one fixed point in a world of changing friendships is that Thomas More will not give in!

MORE (*urgent to explain*): To me it *has* to be, for that's myself! Affection goes as deep in me as you I think, but only God is love right through, Howard; and *that's* my *self*.

NORFOLK: And who are you? Goddammit, man, it's disproportionate! *We're* supposed to be the arrogant ones, the proud, splenetic ones – and we've all given in! Why must you stand out? (*Quiet and quick.*) You'll break my heart.

MORE (*moved*): We'll do it now, Howard: part, as friends, and meet as strangers. (*He attempts to take* NORFOLK'S *hand.*)

NORFOLK (*throwing it off*): Daft, Thomas! Why d'you want to take your friendship from me? For friendship's sake! You say we'll meet as strangers and every word you've said confirms our friendship!

MORE (*takes a last affectionate look at him*): Oh, that can be remedied. (*Walks away, turns: in a tone of deliberate insult.*) Norfolk, you're a fool.

NORFOLK (*starts: then smiles and folds his arms*): You can't place a quarrel; you haven't the style.

MORE: Hear me out. You and your class have 'given in' – as you rightly call it – because the religion of this country means nothing to you one way or the other.

NORFOLK: Well, that's a foolish saying for a start; the nobility of England has always been——

MORE: The nobility of England, my lord, would have snored through the Sermon on the Mount. But you'll labour like Thomas Aquinas over a rat-dog's pedigree. Now what's the name of those distorted creatures you're all breeding at the moment?

NORFOLK (*steadily, but roused towards anger by* MORE'S *tone*): An artificial quarrel's not a quarrel.

MORE: Don't deceive yourself, my lord, we've had a quarrel since the day we met, our friendship was but sloth.

NORFOLK: You can be cruel when you've a mind to be; but I've always known that.

MORE: What's the name of those dogs? Marsh mastiffs? Bog beagles?

NORFOLK: Water spaniels!

MORE: And what would you do with a water spaniel that was afraid of water? You'd hang it! Well, as a spaniel is to water, so is a man to his own self. I will not give in because I oppose it – *I* do – not my pride, not my spleen, nor any other of my appetites but *I* do – *I*! (*He goes up to him and feels him up and down like an animal.* MARGARET'S *voice is heard, well off, call-*

ing her father. MORE's *attention is irresistibly caught by this; but he turns back determinedly to* NORFOLK.) Is there no single sinew in the midst of this that serves no appetite of Norfolk's but is, just, Norfolk? There is! Give *that* some exercise, my lord!

MARGARET (*off, nearer*): Father?

NORFOLK (*breathing hard*): Thomas. . . .

MORE: Because as you stand, you'll go before your Maker in a very ill condition!

Enter MARGARET, *below; she stops, amazed at them.*

NORFOLK: Now steady, Thomas. . . .

MORE: And he'll have to think that somewhere back along your pedigree – a bitch got over the wall!

NORFOLK *lashes out at him; he ducks and winces. Exit* NORFOLK.

MARGARET: Father! (*As he straightens up.*) Father, what was that?

MORE: That was Norfolk. (*Looks after him wistfully.*)

Enter ROPER.

ROPER (*excited, almost gleeful*): Do you know, sir? Have you heard? (MORE *still looking off, unanswering. To* MARGARET. Have you told him?

MARGARET (*gently*): We've been looking for you, Father. (MORE *the same.*)

ROPER: There's to be a new Act through Parliament, sir!

MORE (*half-turning, half attending*): Act?

ROPER: Yes, sir – about the Marriage!

MORE (*indifferent*): Oh. (*Turning back again.*)

ROPER *and* MARGARET *look at one another.*

MARGARET (*puts hand on his arm*): Father, by this Act, they're going to administer an oath.

MORE (*instantaneous attention*): An oath! (*Looks from one to other.*) On what compulsion?

ROPER: It's expected to be treason!

MORE (*very still*): What is the oath?

ROPER (*puzzled*): It's about the Marriage, sir.

MORE: But what is the wording?

ROPER: We don't need to know the (*contemptuous*) wording – we know what it will mean!

MORE: It will mean what the words say! An oath is *made* of words! It may be possible to take it. Or avoid it. Have we a copy of the Bill? (*To* MARGARET.)

MARGARET: There's one coming out from the City.

MORE: Then let's get home and look at it. Oh, I've no boat (*He looks off again after* NORFOLK.)

MARGARET (*gently*): What happened, Father?

MORE: I spoke, slightingly, of water spaniels. Let's get home. (*He turns and sees* ROPER *excited and truculent.*) Now listen, Will. And, Meg, you know I know you well, you listen too. God made the *angels* to show him splendour – as he made animals for innocence and plants for their simplicity. But Man he made to serve him wittily, in the tangle of his mind! If he suffers us to fall to such a case that there is no escaping, then we may stand to our tackle as best we can, and yes, Will, then we may clamour like champions . . . if we have the spittle for it. And no doubt it delights God to see splendour where he only looked for complexity. But it's God's part, not our own, to bring ourselves to that extremity! Our natural business lies in escaping – so let's get home and study this Bill.

    Exit MORE, ROPER *and* MARGARET.

    Enter COMMON MAN, *dragging basket. The rear of the stage remains water-lit in moonlight. Iron grills now descend to cover all the apertures. Also, a rack, which remains suspended, and a cage which is lowered to the floor. While this takes place the* COMMON MAN *arranges three chairs behind a table. Then he turns and watches the completion of the transformation.*

COMMON MAN (*aggrieved*): *Now* look! . . . I don't suppose anyone enjoyed it any more than he did. Well, not much more. (*Takes from basket and dons coat and hat.*) Jailer! (*Shrugs.*)

It's a job. The pay scale being what it is they have to take a rather common type of man into the prison service. But it's a job like any other job. Bit nearer the knuckle than most perhaps.

Enter right, CROMWELL, NORFOLK, CRANMER, *who sit, and* RICH, *who stands behind them. Enter left,* MORE, *who enters the cage and lies down.*

They'd let him out if they could but for various reasons they can't. (*Twirling keys.*) I'd let him out if I could but I can't. Not without taking up residence in there myself. And he's in there already, so what'd be the point? You know the old adage? 'Better a live rat than a dead lion,' and that's about it.

An envelope descends swiftly before him. He opens it and reads: 'With reference to the old adage: Thomas Cromwell was found guilty of High Treason and executed on 28 July 1540. Norfolk was found guilty of High Treason and should have been executed on 27 January 1547 but on the night of 26 January, the King died of syphilis and wasn't able to sign the warrant. Thomas Cranmer.' (*Jerking thumb.*) That's the other one – 'was burned alive on 21 March 1556.' (*He is about to conclude but sees a postscript.*) Oh. 'Richard Rich became a Knight and Solicitor-General, a Baron and Lord Chancellor, and died in his bed.' So did I. And so, I hope (*pushing off basket*) will all of you.

He goes to MORE *and rouses him. Heavy bell strikes one.*

MORE (*rousing*): What, again?

JAILER: Sorry, sir.

MORE (*flops back*): What time is it?

JAILER: Just struck one, sir.

MORE: Oh, this is iniquitous!

JAILER (*anxious*): Sir.

MORE (*sitting up*): All right. (*Putting on slippers.*) Who's there?

JAILER: The Secretary, the Duke, and the Archbishop.

MORE: I'm flattered. (*Stands. Claps hand to hip.*) Ooh! (*Preceded by* JAILER *limps across stage right: he has aged and is pale, but his manner though wary, is relaxed: while that of the Commission is bored, tense, and jumpy.*)

NORFOLK (*looks at him*): A chair for the prisoner. (*While* JAILER *brings a chair and* MORE *sits in it,* NORFOLK *rattles off*): This is the Seventh Commission to enquire into the case of Sir Thomas More, appointed by His Majesty's Council. Have you anything to say?

MORE: No. (*To* JAILER.) Thank you.

NORFOLK (*sitting back*): Mr Secretary.

CROMWELL: Sir Thomas – (*breaks off*) – do the witnesses attend?

RICH: Mr Secretary.

JAILER: Sir.

CROMWELL (*to* JAILER): Nearer! (*He advances a bit.*) Come where you can hear! (JAILER *takes up stance by* RICH. *To* MORE.) Sir Thomas, you have seen this document before?

MORE: Many times.

CROMWELL: It is the Act of Succession. These are the names of those who have sworn to it.

MORE: I have, as you say, seen it before.

CROMWELL: Will you swear to it?

MORE: No.

NORFOLK: Thomas, we must know plainly——

CROMWELL (*throws down document*): Your Grace, *please*!

NORFOLK: Master Cromwell! (*They regard one another in hatred.*)

CROMWELL: I beg Your Grace's pardon. (*Sighing, rests head in hands.*)

NORFOLK: Thomas, we must know plainly whether you recognise the offspring of Queen Anne as heirs to His Majesty.

MORE: The King in Parliament tells me that they are. Of course I recognise them.

NORFOLK: Will you swear that you do?

MORE: Yes.

NORFOLK: Then why won't you swear to the Act?

CROMWELL (*impatient*): Because there is more than that *in* the Act.

NORFOLK: Is that it?

MORE (*after a pause*): Yes.

NORFOLK: Then we must find out what it is in the Act that he objects to!

CROMWELL: Brilliant. (NORFOLK *rounds on him.*)

CRANMER (*hastily*): Your Grace—— May I try?

NORFOLK: Certainly. I've no pretension to be an expert, in Police work.

> *During next speech* CROMWELL *straightens up and folds arms resignedly.*

CRANMER (*clears throat fussily*): Sir Thomas, it states in the preamble that the King's former marriage, to the Lady Catherine, was unlawful, she being previously his brother's wife and the – er – 'Pope' having no authority to sanction it. (*Gently.*) Is that what you deny? (*No reply.*) Is that what you dispute? (*No reply.*) Is that what you are not sure of? (*No reply.*)

NORFOLK: Thomas, you insult the King and His Council in the person of the Lord Archbishop!

MORE: I insult no one. I will not take the oath. I will not tell you why I will not.

NORFOLK: Then your reasons must be treasonable!

MORE: Not 'must be'; may be.

NORFOLK: It's a fair assumption!

MORE: The law requires more than an assumption; the law requires a fact. (CROMWELL *looks at him and away again.*)

CRANMER: I cannot judge your legal standing in the case; but until I know the *ground* of your objections, I can only guess your spiritual standing too.

MORE (*is for a second furiously affronted; then humour overtakes him*): If you're willing to guess at that, Your Grace, it should be a small matter to guess my objections.

CROMWELL (*quickly*): You do have objections to the Act?

NORFOLK (*happily*): Well, we know *that*, Cromwell!

MORE: You don't, my lord. You may *suppose* I have objections. All you *know* is that I will not swear to it. From sheer delight to give you trouble it might be.

NORFOLK: Is it material why you won't?

MORE: It's most material. For refusing to swear my goods are forfeit and I am condemned to life imprisonment. You cannot lawfully harm me further. But if you were right in supposing I had reasons for refusing and right again in supposing my reasons to be treasonable, the law would let you cut my head off.

NORFOLK (*he has followed with some difficulty*): Oh yes.

CROMWELL (*admiring murmur*): Oh, well done, Sir Thomas. I've been trying to make that clear to His Grace for some time.

NORFOLK (*hardly responds to the insult; his face is gloomy and disgusted*): Oh, confound all this. . . . (*With real dignity.*) I'm not a scholar, as Master Cromwell never tires of pointing out, and frankly I don't know whether the marriage was lawful or not. But damn it, Thomas, look at those names. . . . You know those men! Can't you do what I did, and come with us, for fellowship?

MORE (*moved*): And when we stand before God, and you are sent to Paradise for doing according to your conscience, and I am damned for not doing according to mine, will you come with me, for fellowship?

CRANMER: So those of us whose names are there are damned. Sir Thomas?

MORE: I don't know, Your Grace. I have no window to look into another man's conscience. I condemn no one.

CRANMER: Then the matter is capable of question?

MORE: Certainly.

CRANMER: But that you owe obedience to your King is not

capable of question. So weigh a doubt against a certainty –
and sign.

MORE: Some men think the Earth is round, others think it flat;
it is a matter capable of question. But if it is flat, will the
King's command make it round? And if it is round, will the
King's command flatten it? No, I will not sign.

CROMWELL (*leaping up, with ceremonial indignation*): Then you
have more regard to your own doubt than you have to his
command!

MORE: For myself, I have no doubt.

CROMWELL: No doubt of what?

MORE: No doubt of my grounds for refusing this oath.
Grounds I will tell to the King alone, and which you, Mr
Secretary, will not trick out of me.

NORFOLK: Thomas——

MORE: Oh, gentlemen, can't I go to bed?

CROMWELL: You don't seem to appreciate the seriousness of
your position.

MORE: I defy anyone to live in that cell for a year and not
appreciate the seriousness of his position.

CROMWELL: Yet the State has harsher punishments.

MORE: You threaten like a dockside bully.

CROMWELL: How should I threaten?

MORE: Like a Minister of State, with justice!

CROMWELL: Oh, justice is what you're threatened with.

MORE: Then I'm not threatened.

NORFOLK: Master Secretary, I think the prisoner may retire as
he requests. Unless you, my lord——?

CRANMER (*pettish*): No, I see no purpose in prolonging the
interview.

NORFOLK: Then good night, Thomas.

MORE (*hesitates*): Might I have one or two more books?

CROMWELL: You have books?

MORE: Yes.

CROMWELL: I didn't know; you shouldn't have.

MORE (*turns to go: pauses. Desperately*): May I see my family?

CROMWELL: No! (MORE *returns to cell.*) Jailer!

JAILER: Sir!

CROMWELL: Have you ever heard the prisoner speak of the King's divorce, or the King's Supremacy of the Church, or the King's marriage?

JAILER: No, sir, not a word.

CROMWELL: If he does, you will of course report it to the Lieutenant.

JAILER: Of course, sir.

CROMWELL: You will swear an oath to that effect.

JAILER (*cheerfully*): Certainly, sir!

CROMWELL: Archbishop?

CRANMER (*laying cross of vestment on table*): Place your left hand on this and raise your right hand – take your hat off—— Now say after me: I swear by my immortal soul – (JAILER *overlapping, repeats the oath with him*) that I will report truly anything said by Sir Thomas More against the King the Council or the State of the Realm. So help me God. Amen.

JAILER (*overlapping*): So help me God. Amen.

CROMWELL: And there's fifty guineas in it if you do.

JAILER (*looks at him gravely*): Yes, sir. (*And goes.*)

CRANMER (*hastily*): That's not to tempt you into perjury, my man!

JAILER: No, sir! (*At exit pauses; to audience.*) Fifty guineas isn't tempting; fifty guineas is alarming. If he'd left it at swearing. . . . But fifty—— That's serious money. If it's worth that much now it's worth my neck presently. (*Decision.*) I want no part of it. They can sort it out between them. I feel my deafness coming on.

   Exit JAILER. *The Commission rises.*

CROMWELL: Rich!

RICH: Secretary?

CROMWELL: Tomorrow morning, remove the prisoner's books.

NORFOLK: Is that necessary?

CROMWELL (*suppressed exasperation*): Norfolk. With regards this case, the King is becoming impatient.

NORFOLK: Aye, with you.

CROMWELL: With all of us. (*He walks over to the rack.*) You know the King's impatience, how commodious it is!

    NORFOLK *and* CRANMER *exit.* CROMWELL *is brooding over the instrument of torture.*

RICH: Secretary!

CROMWELL (*abstracted*): Yes . . . ?

RICH: Sir Redvers Llewellyn has retired.

CROMWELL (*not listening*): Mm . . . ?

RICH (*goes to other end of rack and faces him. Some indignation*): The Attorney-General for Wales. His post is vacant. You said I might approach you.

CROMWELL (*contemptuous impatience*): Oh, not *now*. . . . (*Broods.*) He must submit, the alternatives are bad. While More's alive the King's conscience breaks into fresh stinking flowers every time he gets from bed. And if I bring about More's death – I plant my own, I think. There's no other good solution! He must submit! (*He whirls the windlass of the rack, producing a startling clatter from the ratchet. They look at each other. He turns it again slowly, shakes his head and lets go.*) No; the King will not permit it. (*Walks away.*) We have to find some gentler way.

    The scene change commences as he says this and exit RICH *and* CROMWELL. *From night it becomes morning, cold grey light from off the grey water. And enter* JAILER *and* MARGARET.

JAILER: Wake up, Sir Thomas! Your family's here!

MORE (*starting up. A great cry*): Margaret! What's this? You can visit me? (*Thrusts arms through cage.*) Meg. Meg. (*She goes to him. Then horrified.*) For God's sake, Meg, they've not put *you* in here?

JAILER (*reassuring*): No-o-o, sir. Just a visit; a short one.

MORE (*excited*): Jailer, jailer, let me out of this.

JAILER (*stolid*): Yes, sir. I'm allowed to let you out.

MORE: Thank you. (*Goes to door of cage, gabbling while* JAILER *unlocks it.*) Thank you, thank you. (*Comes out. He and she regard each other; then she drops into a curtsey.*)

MARGARET: Good morning, Father.

MORE (*ecstatic, wraps her to him*): Oh, good morning—— Good morning. (*Enter* ALICE, *supported by* WILL. *She, like* MORE, *has aged and is poorly dressed.*) Good morning, Alice. Good morning, Will.

ROPER *is staring at the rack in horror.* ALICE *approaches* MORE *and peers at him technically.*

ALICE (*almost accusatory*): Husband, how do you do?

MORE (*smiling over* MARGARET): As well as need be, Alice. Very happy now. Will?

ROPER: This is an awful place!

MORE: Except it's keeping me from you, my dears, it's not so bad. Remarkably like any other place.

ALICE (*looks up critically*): It drips!

MORE: Yes. Too near the river. (ALICE *goes apart and sits, her face bitter.*)

MARGARET (*disengages from him, takes basket from her mother*): We've brought you some things. (*Shows him. There is constraint between them.*) Some cheese. . . .

MORE: Cheese.

MARGARET: And a custard. . . .

MORE: A custard!

MARGARET: And, these other things. . . . (*She doesn't look at him.*)

ROPER: And a bottle of wine. (*Offering it.*)

MORE: Oh. (*Mischievous.*) Is it good, son Roper?

ROPER: I don't know, sir.

MORE (*looks at them, puzzled*): Well.

ROPER: Sir, come out! Swear to the Act! Take the oath and come out!

MORE: Is this why they let you come?

ROPER: Yes . . . Meg's under oath to persuade you.

MORE (*coldly*): That was silly, Meg. How did you come to do that?

MARGARET: I wanted to!

MORE: You want me to swear to the Act of Succession?

MARGARET: 'God more regards the thoughts of the heart than the words of the mouth' or so you've always told me.

MORE: Yes.

MARGARET: Then say the words of the oath and in your heart think otherwise.

MORE: What is an oath then but words we say to God?

MARGARET: That's very neat.

MORE: Do you mean it isn't true?

MARGARET: No, it's true.

MORE: Then it's a poor argument to call it 'neat', Meg. When a man takes an oath, Meg, he's holding his own self in his own hands. Like water (*cups hands*) and if he opens his fingers *then* – he needn't hope to find himself again. Some men aren't capable of this, but I'd be loathe to think your father one of them.

MARGARET: So should I. . . .

MORE: Then——

MARGARET: There's something else I've been thinking.

MORE: Oh, Meg!

MARGARET: In any state that was half good, you would be raised up high, not here, for what you've done already.

MORE: All right.

MARGARET: It's not your fault the State's three-quarters bad.

MORE: No.

MARGARET: Then if you elect to suffer for it, you elect yourself a hero.

MORE: That's very neat. But look now . . . If we lived in a State where virtue was profitable, common sense would make us good, and greed would make us saintly. And we'd live like animals or angels in the happy land that *needs* no heroes. But since in fact we see that avarice, anger, envy, pride, sloth, lust and stupidity commonly profit far beyond humility, chastity, fortitude, justice and thought, and have to choose, to be human at all . . . why then perhaps we *must* stand fast a little – even at the risk of being heroes.

MARGARET (*emotional*): But in reason! Haven't you done as much as God can reasonably *want*?

MORE: Well . . . finally . . . it isn't a matter of reason; finally it's a matter of love.

ALICE (*hostile*): You're content then, to be shut up here with mice and rats when you might be home with us!

MORE (*flinching*): Content? If they'd open a crack that wide (*between finger and thumb*) I'd be through it. (*To* MARGARET.) Well, has Eve run out of apples?

MARGARET: I've not yet told you what the house is like, without you.

MORE: Don't, Meg.

MARGARET: What we do in the evenings, now that you're not there.

MORE: Meg, have done!

MARGARET: We sit in the dark because we've no candles. And we've no talk because we're wondering what they're doing to you here.

MORE: The King's more merciful than you. He doesn't use the rack.

    Enter JAILER.

JAILER: Two minutes to go, sir. I thought you'd like to know.

MORE: Two minutes!

JAILER: Till seven o'clock, sir. Sorry. Two minutes.

    Exit JAILER.

MORE: Jailer——! (*Seizes* ROPER *by the arm*.) Will – go to him, talk to him, keep him occupied—— (*Propelling him after* JAILER.)

ROPER: How, sir?

MORE: Anyhow! – Have you got any money?

ROPER (*eager*): Yes!

MORE: No, don't try and bribe him! Let him play for it; he's got a pair of dice. And talk to him, you understand! And take this (*the wine*) – and mind you share it – do it properly, Will! (ROPER *nods vigorously and exit*.) Now listen, you must leave the country. All of you must leave the country.

MARGARET: And leave you here?

MORE: It makes no difference, Meg; they won't let you see me again. (*Breathlessly, a prepared speech under pressure.*) You must all go on the same day, but not on the same boat; different boats from different ports——

MARGARET: After the trial, then.

MORE: There'll be no trial, they have no case. Do this for me I beseech you?

MARGARET: Yes.

MORE: Alice? (*She turns her back.*) Alice, I command it!

ALICE (*harshly*): Right!

MORE (*looks into basket*): Oh, this is splendid; I know who packed this.

ALICE (*harshly*): I packed it.

MORE: Yes. (*Eats a morsel.*) You still make superlative custard, Alice.

ALICE: Do I?

MORE: That's a nice dress you have on.

ALICE: It's my cooking dress.

MORE: It's very nice anyway. Nice colour.

ALICE (*turns. Quietly*): By God, you think very little of me. (*Mounting bitterness.*) I know I'm a fool. But I'm no such fool as at this time to be lamenting for my dresses! Or to relish complimenting on my custard!

MORE (*regarding her with frozen attention. He nods once or twice*): I am well rebuked. (*Holds out his hands.*) Al——!

ALICE: No! (*She remains where she is, glaring at him.*)

MORE (*he is in great fear of her*): I am faint when I think of the worst that they may do to me. But worse than that would be to go, with you not understanding why I go.

ALICE: I don't!

MORE (*just hanging on to his self-possession*): Alice, if you can tell
    me that you understand, I think I can make a good death, if
    I have to.

ALICE: Your death's no 'good' to me!

MORE: Alice, you must tell me that you understand!

ALICE: I don't! (*She throws it straight at his head.*) I don't believe
    this had to happen.

MORE (*his face is drawn*): If you say that, Alice, I don't see how
    I'm to face it.

ALICE: It's the truth!

MORE (*gasping*): You're an honest woman.

ALICE: Much good may it do me! I'll tell you what I'm afraid
    of; that when you've gone, I shall hate you for it.

MORE (*turns from her: his face working*): Well, you mustn't,
    Alice, that's all. (*Swiftly she crosses the stage to him; he turns
    and they clasp each other fiercely*). You mustn't, you——

ALICE (*covers his mouth with her hand*): S-s-sh. . . . As for under-
    standing, I understand you're the best man that I ever met or
    am likely to; and if you go – well God knows why I suppose
    – though as God's my witness God's kept deadly quiet about
    it! And if anyone wants my opinion of the King and his
    Council they've only to ask for it!

MORE: Why, it's a lion I married! A lion! A lion! (*He breaks
    away from her his face shining.*) Get them to take half this to
    Bishop Fisher – they've got him in the upper gallery——

ALICE: It's for you, not Bishop Fisher!

MORE: Now do as I ask—— (*Breaks off a piece of the custard and
    eats it.*) Oh, it's good, it's very, very good. (*He puts his face
    in his hands;* ALICE *and* MARGARET *comfort him;* ROPER *and
    JAILER *erupt on to the stage above, wrangling fiercely.*)

JAILER: It's no good, sir! I know what you're up to! And it
    can't be done!

ROPER: Another minute, man!

JAILER (*to* MORE *descending*): Sorry, sir, time's up!

ROPER (*gripping his shoulder from behind*): For pity's sake—!

JAILER (*shaking him off*): Now don't do that, sir! Sir Thomas, the ladies will have to go now!

MORE: You said seven o'clock!

JAILER: It's seven now. You must understand my position, sir.

MORE: But one more minute!

MARGARET: Only a little while – give us a little while!

JAILER (*reproving*): Now, Miss, you don't want to get me into trouble.

ALICE: Do as you're told. Be off at once!

The first stroke of seven is heard on a heavy, deliberate bell, which continues, reducing what follows to a babble.

JAILER (*taking* MARGARET *firmly by the upper arm*): Now come along, Miss; you'll get your father into trouble as well as me. (ROPER *descends and grabs him.*) Are you obstructing me, sir? (MARGARET *embraces* MORE, *and dashes up the stairs and exit, followed by* ROPER. *Taking* ALICE *gingerly by the arm.*) Now, my lady, no trouble!

ALICE (*throwing him off as she rises*): Don't put your muddy hand on me!

JAILER: Am I to call the guard then? Then come on!

ALICE, facing him, puts foot on bottom stair and so retreats before him, backwards.

MORE: For God's sake, man, we're saying good-bye!

JAILER: You don't know what you're asking, sir. You don't know how you're watched.

ALICE: Filthy, stinking, gutter-bred turnkey!

JAILER: Call me what you like, ma'am; you've got to go.

ALICE: I'll see you suffer for this!

JAILER: You're doing your husband no good!

MORE: Alice, good-bye, my love!

On this, the last stroke of the seven sounds. ALICE *raises her hand, turns, and with considerable dignity, exit.* JAILER *stops at head of stairs and addresses* MORE, *who, still crouching, turns from him, facing audience.*

JAILER (*reasonably*): You understand my position, sir, there's nothing I can do; I'm a plain simple man and just want to keep out of trouble.

MORE (*cries out passionately*): Oh, Sweet Jesus! These plain, simple, men!

Immediately: (1) *Music, portentous and heraldic.*

(2) *Bars, rack and cage flown swiftly upwards.*

(3) *Lighting change from cold grey to warm yellow, re-creating a warm interior.*

(4) *Several narrow panels, scarlet and bearing the monogram 'HR VIII' in gold are lowered. Also an enormous Royal Coat-of-Arms which hangs above the table stage right.*

(5) *The* JAILER, *doffing costume comes down the stairs and:*

(A) *Places a chair for the Accused, helps* MORE *to it, and gives him a scroll which he studies.*

(B) *Fetches from the wings his prop basket, and produces: (I) A large hour-glass and papers which he places on table, stage right. (II) Twelve folding stools which he arranges in two rows of six each. While he is still doing this, and just before the panels and Coat-of-Arms have finished their descent, enter* CROMWELL. *He ringingly addresses the audience (while the* COMMON MAN *is still bustling about his chores) as soon as the music ends, which it does at this point, on a fanfare.*

CROMWELL (*indicating descending props*):

> What Englishman can behold without Awe.
> The Canvas and the Rigging of the Law!
> (*Brief fanfare.*)
> Forbidden here the galley-master's whip—
> Hearts of Oak, in the Law's Great Ship!
> (*Brief fanfare.*)

(*To* COMMON MAN *who is tiptoeing discreetly off stage.*) Where are you going?

COMMON MAN: I've finished here, sir.

Above the two rows of stools the COMMON MAN *has suspended from two wires, supported by two pairs of sticks, two rows of hats for the presumed occupants. Seven are plain grey hats, four are those worn by the* STEWARD, BOATMAN, INNKEEPER *and* JAILER. *And the last is another of the plain grey ones. The basket remains on stage, clearly visible.*

CROMWELL: You're the Foreman of the Jury.

COMMON MAN: Oh no, sir.

CROMWELL: You are John Dauncey. A general dealer?

COMMON MAN (*gloomy*): Yes, sir?

CROMWELL (*resuming his rhetorical stance*): Foreman of the Jury. Does the cap fit?

COMMON MAN *puts on the grey hat. It fits.*

COMMON MAN: Yes, sir.

CROMWELL (*resuming rhetorical stance*):

> So, now we'll apply the good, plain sailor's art,
> And fix these quicksands on the Law's plain chart!

Renewed, more prolonged fanfare, during which enter CRANMER *and* NORFOLK, *who stand behind the table stage right. On their entry* MORE *and* FOREMAN *rise. So soon as fanfare is finished* NORFOLK *speaks.*

NORFOLK (*takes refuge behind a rigorously official manner*): Sir Thomas More, you are called before us here at the Hall of Westminster to answer charge of High Treason. Nevertheless, and though you have heinously offended the King's Majesty, we hope if you will even now forthink and repent of your obstinate opinions, you may still taste his gracious pardon.

MORE: My lords, I thank you. Howbeit I make my petition to Almighty God that he will keep me in this, my honest mind to the last hour that I shall live. . . . As for the matters you may charge me with, I fear, from my present weakness, that neither my wit nor my memory will serve to make sufficient answers. . . . I should be glad to sit down.

NORFOLK: Be seated. Master Secretary Cromwell, have you the charge?

CROMWELL: I have, my lord.

NORFOLK: Then read the charge.

CROMWELL (*approaching* MORE, *behind him, with papers; informally*): It is the same charge, Sir Thomas, that was brought against Bishop Fisher. . . . (*As one who catches himself up punctiliously.*) The *late* Bishop Fisher I should have said.

MORE (*tonelessly*): 'Late'?

CROMWELL: Bishop Fisher was executed this morning.

MORE'S *face expresses violent shock, then grief; he turns his head away from* CROMWELL *who is observing him clinically.*

NORFOLK: Master Secretary, read the charge!

CROMWELL (*formal*): That you did conspire traitorously and maliciously to deny and deprive our liege lord Henry of his undoubted certain title, Supreme Head of the Church in England.

MORE (*surprise, shock, and indignation*): But I have never denied this title!

CROMWELL: You refused the oath tendered to you at the Tower and elsewhere——

MORE (*the same*): Silence is not denial. And for my silence I am punished, with imprisonment. Why have I been called again? (*At this point he is sensing that the trial has been in some way rigged.*)

NORFOLK: On a charge of High Treason, Sir Thomas.

CROMWELL: For which the punishment is *not* imprisonment.

MORE: Death . . . comes for us all, my lords. Yes, even for Kings he comes, to whom amidst all their Royalty and brute strength he will neither kneel nor make them any reverence nor pleasantly desire them to come forth, but roughly grasp them by the very breast and rattle them until they be stark dead! So causing their bodies to be buried in a pit and sending *them* to a judgement . . . whereof at their death their success is uncertain.

CROMWELL: Treason enough here!

NORFOLK: The death of Kings is not in question, Sir Thomas,

MORE: Nor mine, I trust, until I'm proven guilty.

NORFOLK (*leaning forward urgently*): Your life lies in your own hand, Thomas, as it always has.

MORE (*absorbs this*): For our own deaths, my lord, yours and mine, dare we for shame desire to enter the Kingdom with ease, when Our Lord Himself entered with so much pain?

And now he faces CROMWELL *his eyes sparkling with suspicion.*

CROMWELL: Now, Sir Thomas, you stand upon your silence.

MORE: I do.

CROMWELL: But, Gentlemen of the Jury, there are many kinds of silence. Consider first the silence of a man when he is dead. Let us say we go into the room where he is lying; and let us say it is in the dead of night – there's nothing like darkness for sharpening the ear; and we listen. What do we hear? Silence. What does it betoken, this silence? Nothing. This is silence, pure and simple. But consider another case. Suppose I were to draw a dagger from my sleeve and make to kill the prisoner with it, and suppose their lordships there, instead of crying out for me to stop or crying out for help to stop me, maintained their silence. That *would* betoken! It would betoken a willingness that I should do it, and under the law they would be guilty with me. So silence can, according to circumstances, speak. Consider, now, the circumstances of the prisoner's silence. The oath was put to good and faithful subjects up and down the country and they had declared His Grace's Title to be just and good. And when it came to the prisoner he refused. He calls this silence. Yet is there a man in this court, is there a man in this country, who does not *know* Sir Thomas More's opinion of this title? Of course not! But how can that be? Because this silence betokened – nay this silence *was* – not silence at all, but most eloquent denial.

MORE (*with some of the academic's impatience for a shoddy line of reasoning*): Not so, Mr Secretary, the maxim is 'qui tacet consentire'. (*Turns to* COMMON MAN.) The maxim of the law is: (*very carefully*) 'Silence Gives Consent'. If therefore, you wish to construe what my silence 'betokened', you must construe that I consented, not that I denied.

CROMWELL: Is that what the world in fact construes from it? Do you pretend that is what you *wish* the world to construe from it?

MORE: The world must construe according to its wits. This Court must construe according to the law.

CROMWELL: I put it to the Court that the prisoner is perverting the law – making smoky what should be a clear light to discover to the Court his own wrongdoing! (CROMWELL'S *official indignation is slipping into genuine anger and* MORE *responds.*)

MORE: The law is not a 'light' for you or any man to see by; the law is not an instrument of any kind. (*To the* FOREMAN.) The law is a causeway upon which so long as he keeps to it a citizen may walk safely. (*Earnestly addressing him.*) In matters of conscience——

CROMWELL (*bitterly smiling*): The conscience, the conscience...

MORE (*turning*): The word is not familiar to you?

CROMWELL: By God, too familiar! I am very used to hear it in the mouths of criminals!

MORE: I am used to hear bad men misuse the name of God, yet God exists. (*Turning back.*) In matters of conscience, the loyal subject is more bounden to be loyal *to* his conscience than to any other thing.

CROMWELL (*breathing hard: straight at* MORE): – And so provide a noble motive for his frivolous self-conceit!

MORE (*earnestly*): It is not so, Master Cromwell – very and pure necessity for respect of my own soul.

CROMWELL: – Your own self you mean!

MORE: Yes, a man's soul is his self!

CROMWELL (*thrusts his face into* MORE'*s. They hate each other and each other's standpoint*): A miserable thing, whatever you call it, that lives like a bat in a Sunday School! A shrill incessant pedagogue about its own salvation – but nothing to say of your place in the State! Under the King! In a great native country!

MORE (*not untouched*): Can I help my King by giving him lies when he asks for truth? Will you help England by populating her with liars?

CROMWELL (*backs away. His face stiff with malevolence*): My lords, I wish to call (*raises voice*) Sir Richard Rich!

Enter RICH. *He is now splendidly official, in dress and bearing; even* NORFOLK *is a bit impressed.*

Sir Richard (*indicating* CRANMER).

CRANMER (*proffering Bible*): I do solemnly swear . . .

RICH: I do solemnly swear that the evidence I shall give before the Court shall be the truth, the whole truth, and nothing but the truth.

CRANMER (*discreetly*): So help me God, Sir Richard.

RICH: So help me God.

NORFOLK: Take your stand there, Sir Richard.

CROMWELL: Now, Rich, on 12 March, you were at the Tower?

RICH: I was.

CROMWELL: With what purpose?

RICH: I was sent to carry away the prisoner's books.

CROMWELL: Did you talk with the prisoner?

RICH: Yes.

CROMWELL: Did you talk about the King's Supremacy of the Church?

RICH: Yes.

CROMWELL: What did you say?

RICH: I said to him: 'Supposing there was an Act of Parliament to say that I, Richard Rich, were to be King, would not you, Master More, take me for King?' 'That I would,' he said, 'for then you would be King.'

CROMWELL: Yes?

RICH: Then he said——

NORFOLK (*sharply*): The prisoner?

RICH: Yes, my lord. 'But I will put you a higher case,' he said. 'How if there were an Act of Parliament to say that God should not be God?'

MORE: This is true; and then you said——

NORFOLK: Silence! Continue.

RICH: I said 'Ah, but I will put you a middle case. Parliament has made our King Head of the Church. Why will you not accept him?'

NORFOLK (*strung up*): Well?

RICH: Then he said Parliament had no power to do it.

NORFOLK: Repeat the prisoner's words!

RICH: He said 'Parliament has not the competence.' Or words to that effect.

CROMWELL: He denied the title?

RICH: He did.

   All look to MORE *but he looks to* RICH.

MORE: In good faith, Rich, I am sorrier for your perjury than my peril.

NORFOLK: Do you deny this?

MORE: Yes! My lords, if I were a man who heeded not the taking of an oath, you know well I need not to be here. Now I will take an oath! If what Master Rich has said is true, then I pray I may never see God in the face! Which I would not say were it otherwise for anything on earth.

CROMWELL (*to* FOREMAN, *calmly, technical*): That is not evidence.

MORE: Is it probable – is it probable – that after so long a silence, on this, the very point so urgently sought of me, I should open my mind to such a man as that?

CROMWELL (*to* RICH): Do you wish to modify your testimony?

RICH: No, Secretary.

MORE: There were two other men! Southwell and Palmer!

CROMWELL: Unhappily, Sir Richard Southwell and Master Palmer are both in Ireland on the King's business. (MORE *gestures helplessly.*) It has no bearing. I have their deposition here in which the Court will see they state that being busy with the prisoner's books they did not hear what was said. (*Hands deposition to* FOREMAN *who examines it with much seriousness.*)

MORE: If I had really said this is it not obvious he would instantly have called these men to witness?

CROMWELL: Sir Richard, have you anything to add?

RICH: Nothing, Mr Secretary.

NORFOLK: Sir Thomas?

MORE (*looking at* FOREMAN): To what purpose? I am a dead man. (*To* CROMWELL.) You have your desire of me. What you have hunted me for is not my actions, but the thoughts of my heart. It is a long road you have opened. For first men will disclaim their hearts and presently they will have no hearts. God help the people whose Statesmen walk your road.

NORFOLK: Then the witness may withdraw.

RICH *crosses stage, watched by* MORE.

MORE: I *have* one question to ask the witness. (RICH *stops.*) That's a chain of office you are wearing. (*Reluctantly* RICH *faces him.*) May I see it? (NORFOLK *motions him to approach.* MORE *examines the medallion.*) The red dragon. (*To* CROMWELL.) What's this?

CROMWELL: Sir Richard is appointed Attorney-General for Wales.

MORE (*looking into* RICH'S *face: with pain and amusement*): For Wales? Why, Richard, it profits a man nothing to give his soul for the whole world. . . . But for Wales——!

Exit RICH, *stiff faced, but infrangibly dignified.*

CROMWELL: Now I must ask the Court's indulgence! I have a message for the prisoner from the King: (*urgent*) Sir Thomas, I am empowered to tell you that even now——

MORE: No no, It cannot be.

CROMWELL: The case rests! (NORFOLK *is staring at* MORE.) My lord!

NORFOLK: The Jury will retire and consider the evidence.

CROMWELL: Considering the evidence it shouldn't be necessary for them to retire. (*Standing over* FOREMAN.) Is it necessary?

FOREMAN *shakes his head.*

NORFOLK: Then is the prisoner guilty or not guilty?

FOREMAN: Guilty, my lord!

NORFOLK (*leaping to his feet; all rise save* MORE): Prisoner at the bar, you have been found guilty of High Treason. The sentence of the Court——

MORE: My lord!

NORFOLK *breaks off.* MORE *has a sly smile. From this point to end of play his manner is of one who has fulfilled all his obligations and will now consult no interests but his own.*

My lord, when *I* was practising the law, the manner was to ask the prisoner *before* pronouncing sentence, if he had anything to say.

NORFOLK (*flummoxed*): Have you anything to say?

MORE: Yes. (*He rises: all others sit.*) To avoid this I have taken every path my winding wits would find. Now that the court has determined to condemn me, God knoweth how, I will discharge my mind . . . concerning my indictment and the King's title. The indictment is grounded in an Act of Parliament which is directly repugnant to the Law of God. The King in Parliament cannot bestow the Supremacy of the Church because it is a Spiritual Supremacy! And more to this the immunity of the Church is promised both in Magna Carta and the King's own Coronation Oath!

CROMWELL: Now we plainly see that you *are* malicious!

MORE: Not so, Mr Secretary! (*He pauses, and launches, very quietly, ruminatively, into his final stock-taking.*) I am the King's true subject, and pray for him and all the realm . . . I do none harm, I say none harm, I think none harm. And if this be not enough to keep a man alive, in good faith I long not to live . . . I have, since I came into prison, been several times in such a case that I thought to die within the hour, and I thank Our Lord I was never sorry for it, but rather sorry when it passed. And therefore, my poor body is at the King's pleasure. Would God my death might do him some good. . . . (*With a great flash of scorn and anger.*) Nevertheless, it is not for the Supremacy that you have sought my blood – but because I would not bend to the marriage!

Immediately scene change commences, while NORFOLK *reads the sentence.*

NORFOLK: Prisoner at the bar, you have been found guilty on the charge of High Treason. The sentence of the Court is that you shall be taken from this Court to the Tower, thence to the place of execution, and there your head shall be stricken from your body, and may God have mercy on your soul!

The scene change is as follows:

(I) *The trappings of justice are flown upwards.*

(II) *The lights are dimmed save for three areas: spots, left and right front, and the arch at the head of the stairs which begins to show blue sky.*

(III) *Through this arch – where the axe and the block are silhouetted against a light of steadily increasing brilliance – comes the murmuration of a large crowd, formalised almost into a chant and mounting, so that* NORFOLK *has to shout the end of his speech.*

In addition to the noise of the crowd and the flying machinery there is stage activity: FOREMAN *doffs cap, and as* COMMON MAN *removes the prisoner's chair and then goes to the spot, left.*

CRANMER *also goes to spot, left.*

MORE *goes to spot, right.*

> WOMAN *enters, up right, and goes to spot, left.*

> NORFOLK *remains where he is.*

> *When these movements are complete – they are made naturally, technically –* CROMWELL *goes and stands in the light streaming down the stairs. He beckons the* COMMON MAN *who leaves spot, left, and joins him.* CROMWELL *points to the head of the stairs.* COMMON MAN *shakes his head and indicates in mime that he has no costume. He drags basket into the light and again indicates that there is no costume in it.* CROMWELL *takes a small black mask from his sleeve and offers it to him. The* COMMON MAN *puts it on, thus, in his black tights, becoming the traditional headsman. He ascends the stairs, straddles his legs and picks up the axe, silhouetted against the bright sky. At once the crowd falls silent.*

> *Exit* CROMWELL, *dragging basket.*

> NORFOLK *joins* MORE *in spot, right.*

NORFOLK : I can come no further, Thomas. (*Proffering goblet.*) Here, drink this.

MORE: My master had easel and gall, not wine, given him to drink. Let me be going.

MARGARET: Father! (*She runs to him in the spot from right and flings herself upon him.*) Father! Father, Father, Father, Father!

MORE: Have patience, Margaret, and trouble not thyself. Death comes for us all; even at our birth (*he holds her head and looks down at it for a moment in recollection*) – even at our birth, death does but stand aside a little. It is the law of nature, and the will of God. (*He disengages from her. Dispassionately.*) You have long known the secrets of my heart.

WOMAN: Sir Thomas! (*He stops.*) Remember me, Sir Thomas? When you were Chancellor, you gave a false judgement against me. Remember that now.

MORE: Woman, you see how I am occupied. (*With sudden decision goes to her in spot, left. Crisply.*) I remember your matter well, and if I had to give sentence now I assure you I should not alter it. You have no injury; so go your ways;

and content yourself; and trouble me not! (*He walks swiftly to the stairs. Then stops, realising that* CRANMER, *carrying his Bible, has followed him. Quite kindly.*) I beseech Your Grace, go back.

Offended, CRANMER *does so. The lighting is now complete, i.e., darkness save for three areas of light, the one at head of stairs now dazzlingly brilliant. When* MORE *gets to head of stairs by the* HEADSMAN *there is a single shout from the crowd. He turns to* HEADSMAN.

Friend, be not afraid of your office. You send me to God.

CRANMER (*envious rather than waspish*): You're very sure of that, Sir Thomas.

MORE (*takes off his hat, revealing the grey disordered hair*): He will not refuse one who is so blithe to go to him. (*Kneeling.*)

Immediately, harsh roar of kettledrums and total blackout at head of stairs. While the drums roar, WOMAN *backs into* CRANMER *and exit together.* NORFOLK *assists* MARGARET *from the stage, which is now 'occupied' only by the two spots left and right front. The drums cease.*

HEADSMAN (*from the darkness*): Behold – the head – of a traitor!

Enter into spots left and right, CROMWELL *and* CHAPUYS. *They stop on seeing one another, arrested in postures of frozen hostility while the light spreads plainly over the stage, which is empty save for themselves.*

Then simultaneously they stalk forward, crossing mid-stage with heads high and averted. But as they approach their exits they pause, hesitate, and slowly turn. Thoughtfully they stroll back towards one another. CROMWELL *raises his head and essays a smile.* CHAPUYS *responds. They link arms and approach the stairs. As they go we hear that they are chuckling. There is nothing sinister or malignant in the sound; rather it is the self-mocking, self-indulgent, rather rueful laughter of men who know what the world is and how to be comfortable in it. As they go,* THE CURTAIN FALLS.

ALTERNATIVE ENDING

In the London production of this play at the Globe Theatre the play ended as follows:

Instead of the CROMWELL *and* CHAPUYS *entrance after the* HEADSMAN'S *line* 'Behold – the head – of a traitor!', *the* COMMON MAN *came to the centre stage, having taken off his mask as the executioner, and said:*

'I'm breathing. . . . Are you breathing too? . . . It's nice isn't it? It isn't difficult to keep alive friends . . . just don't make trouble – or if you must make trouble, make the sort of trouble that's expected. Well, I don't need to tell you that. Good night. If we should bump into one another, recognise me.'

(*Exits*)

CURTAIN

From the New York production
Courtesy Robert Whitehead and Roger L. Stevens

Left to right

GEORGE ROSE as The Common Man
LEO McKERN as Thomas Cromwell

(See page 41.)

From the New York production
Courtesy Robert Whitehead and Roger L. Stevens

Left to right

ALBERT DEKKER as The Duke of Norfolk
PETER BRANDON as William Roper
OLGA BELLIN as Margaret More
PAUL SCOFIELD as Sir Thomas More
CAROL GOODNER as Alice More

(See page 52.)

From the New York production
Courtesy Robert Whitehead and Roger L. Stevens

Left to right

PAUL SCOFIELD as Sir Thomas More
LEO McKERN as Thomas Cromwell

(See page 68.)

Left to right

LESTER RAWLINS as The Archbishop of Canterbury
OLGA BELLIN as Margaret More
PAUL SCOFIELD as Sir Thomas More
GEORGE ROSE as The Common Man
SARAH BURTON as The Woman
ALBERT DEKKER as The Duke of Norfolk

(See page 98.)

HISTORICAL BACKGROUND

A Man for All Seasons deals with the last nine years (1526-1535) in the life of Sir Thomas More – a profound administrator, a man of keen intellect, a martyr and saint in the defence of his faith. Born into the midst of that chaos known as the Wars of the Roses, More lived to see the waning power of the Pope in England and the growing authority of the House of Tudor. As a loyal Englishman he did not object to the latter, but as a dutiful son of the Church he could not countenance the former. And in this bitter clash of interests his destruction became inevitable.

The crisis in the affairs of the Royal House and of More arose from the King's not having, after nearly twenty years of marriage to Catherine of Aragon, a son upon whom to settle the succession. Henry began to long for a divorce. Unfortunately, a papal dispensation was necessary, and, though there had been precedents, such a dispensation was not easily obtained. Because Catherine had been the wife of Henry's older brother, the King now argued – and with a text from Holy Writ – that the marriage had never been valid.

Other reasons urged the divorce. Henry's relations with Spain were deteriorating, and Catherine, the aunt of the Spanish king, was no longer politically useful; Henry was in love with Anne Boleyn; he feared a return of the turmoil of the previous century; there now seemed little likelihood that Catherine would produce a male heir; and God's disapproval of the marriage seemed implicit in her failure to do so. All these arguments were, no doubt, in the King's mind when, upon solely theological grounds, he petitioned the Pope.

But the papal territories were then being menaced by the forces of Spain, and Pope Clement VII, for reasons now judged both political and spiritual, refused to accede to Henry's request. In the seemingly interminable negotiations, Cardinal Wolsey, Henry's great chancellor and the last of England's prelate-statesmen, fell from royal favour and Sir Thomas More replaced him.

As a devout Roman Catholic, More also could not condone Henry's course, but the King was adamant. Disregarding the Pope's refusal, he compelled the clergy to submit to his will, to acknowledge him as "the Supreme Head of the Church in England" with, for many, the saving clause, "so far as the law of Christ allows".

Swiftly the King moved to divorce Catherine and marry Anne. In March, 1534, the Act of Succession vested the crown in the new queen's issue; it added a section denying the authority of any "foreign potentate" and demanding from the clergy a full renunciation of the Pope. In November of the same year, Parliament officially passed the Act of Supremacy and established as high treason any attempt "to maliciously deny" any of the royal titles.

In 1532, at the time of the Submission of the Clergy, More had resigned the chancellorship. Henry had accepted the resignation, and for two years Sir Thomas lived in relatively impoverished and peaceful retirement. But he was too powerful a figure to be ignored. The reluctance of this great man to follow the new ways shone as a symbol to all Europe that perhaps — just perhaps — the new ways were not the best ways. Called before the King's Commissioners, he willingly subscribed to the Act of Succession as it bore upon the offspring of Queen Anne, but he steadfastly refused to deny the authority of the Pope. And, though he would offer no reason for his course, he refused also to take the oath demanded by the Act of Supremacy.

Caught between his political loyalty to the Crown and his spiritual loyalty to the Church, More was doomed.

He was accused of yielding to bribery, of complicity in the imposture of the "Holy Maid of Kent", of influencing the stubborn actions of Bishop Fisher. He successfully denied all three charges, and for a short time his position seemed unassailable. Then, through the perjury of Rich, the Solicitor-General, he was at last found guilty of high treason and sentenced to be hanged. On the day assigned for this barbarous act, Henry commuted the sentence to the less-horrible beheading.

To the last moment of his life, More preserved his wit and his dignity. With his death Henry had lost a skilled administrator and an incorruptible subject, but the Church for which More had given his life had gained a martyr and a saint.

NOTES

ACT ONE

PAGE 1. *a big property basket:* a hamper containing the smaller pieces of equipment (or "props") used in the play. Its presence upon the stage foreshadows the role of the Common Man.

speaking costumes: garb which reveals the speakers' importance.

embroidered mouths: mouths capable of more elaborate speech than that of the Common Man.

Old Adam: the first man of *Genesis* and, hence, all men.

The Household Steward: Note that with a quick, fluid shift the Comman Man becomes a character within the action of the play.

on set: the house of Sir Thomas More in Chelsea, a borough of modern London. More settled here about 1524.

PAGE 2. *Sir Thomas More:* born in 1478, the son of a barrister; at 13, a member of the household of the Archbishop of Canterbury; educated at Oxford; 1494-96, a law student; 1519, a member of the Privy Council; 1521, knighted; 1523, Speaker of the House of Commons. At this point in the play, More is a man of great importance, an intimate of the King.

Rich: Richard Rich (1496-1567); educated at Cambridge; a student of the Middle Temple (law); held many minor commissions; 1535, Solicitor-General; 1536, a member of the Privy Council; and Lord Chancellor (1548-51). Historians condemn Rich as a time-server of little real merit. It is important to note that his opening comment takes on great significance as the play advances.

bricks and mortar: buildings or estates.

I thought you were being profound: Rich has referred to physical pain and the mere release from torture. How does More's comment suggest that, even here, the thought of martyrdom is present?

Signor Machiavelli: Niccolo Machiavelli (1469-1527), Florentine writer whose book, *The Prince*, sets forth political principles of craftiness and duplicity. It has been called "the Handbook of Dictators".

PAGE 3. *Master Cromwell:* Thomas Cromwell (1485-1540) began his career as an adventurer upon the Continent; employed by Wolsey (c. 1520); retained his importance after Wolsey's fall; 1531, a member of the Privy Council; 1533, Chancellor of the Exchequer; a member of Parliament — where he acted as Henry's "agent"; knighted in 1536; chief agent in the dissolution of the monasteries. Finally all turned against the "upstart"; he was accused of high treason and beheaded in 1540.

Cardinal's outer doorman: These lines draw attention to the great pomp and wealth of Wolsey, and to the difficulty of gaining an audience with him.

the Duke of Norfolk: Thomas Howard, earl of Surrey and third Duke of Norfolk (1473-1554), was Wolsey's implacable enemy. He was a supporter of the King's divorce. Significantly, Anne Boleyn was his niece. Some historians regard him as little more than the tool of the King. He remained a sympathetic friend of Sir Thomas More until the latter's resistance to the new order was carried, in the Duke's mind, to absurd lengths.

The Dean of St. Paul's: John Colet (1467-1519) became the Dean of St. Paul's Cathedral in 1501. The reference here is intentionally anachronistic.

fifty pounds a year: Real money in this period is quoted by authorities as being fifteen to twenty times its present value.

PAGE 4. *the new school:* With wealth inherited from his father, Colet became responsible for the re-establishment of St. Paul's School (1508-12).

the Court of Requests: This instrument of law was established by Cardinal Wolsey and was popularly known as "the Court of Poor Men's Causes".

PAGE 5. *I was commanded into office:* At the command of the King, More became Master of Requests in 1518.

he stooped: He swooped. Falconry was a highly developed sport of the nobility of the period.

Alice: More's second wife was the widow of John Middleton, a merchant. She and More were married in 1511 and had no children. With greater wit than rancour, he said of her that, when they married, she was "neither a pearl nor a girl".

Margaret: More's eldest daughter (1505-44) was said to be a woman of sympathetic nature, lively, unusually well-educated, capable of disputing philosophy. Her father's favourite child, she proved a great consolation to him at the time of his imprisonment.

PAGE 6. *Aristotle:* Greek philosopher (384-322 B.C.) whose opinions were authority at this time.

'sbody: The swearing upon the parts of God's body was a practice of the period. Its very common use would suggest that the oath was not considered a particularly offensive one.

a City Wife: that is, someone of a delicate and pampered nature.

PAGE 7. *The Cardinal's Secretary:* Cromwell actually became Wolsey's secretary in 1525.

a farrier's son: Cromwell's father, Walter, was at various times a blacksmith, brewer, and fuller.

a butcher's son: Wolsey's father was reportedly a butcher; he was also a landowner. What point are Alice and Norfolk making?

PAGE 8. *The King's business:* Significantly, the transactions necessary to procure Henry's divorce from Queen Catherine were popularly referred to as "the King's matter" or "business".

Is there a boat?: At this time travellers in London would use the Thames more commonly than the muddy and dangerous streets.

Richmond: modern borough of Surrey, some nine miles up the river from London.

the New Inn: one of the Inns of Chancery where More himself had boarded as a student.

Hounslow: a district of Middlesex, some twelve miles from London.

PAGE 9. *some day someone's going to ask him for something:* Note that these comments upon More set the stage for and predict the action which follows.

PAGE 10. *Wolsey:* Thomas Cardinal Wolsey (1475-1530) began his court life as chaplain to Henry VII. In 1511, he was taken into the employ of Henry VIII; in 1513, he became a member of the Privy Council; and in 1515, a cardinal. The symbol of ambition, Wolsey hoped to dominate England, and, indeed, the Continent. For years, hated and feared by the nobility and by Parliament, he was the virtual ruler of England. A villain in the eyes of many, he was yet a hero to some. In the entanglements of the divorce proceedings, he fell from power. At this point in the play, Wolsey fits his description in Samuel Johnson's poem, "The Vanity of Human Wishes":

> In full-blown dignity, see Wolsey stand,
> Law in his voice, and fortune in his hand;
> To him the church, the realm, their pow'rs consign,
> Thro' him the rays of regal bounty shine,
> Turn'd by his nod the stream of honour flows,
> His smile alone security bestows.

the Latin dispatch: All official letters at this time were in Latin. Wolsey shows More a confidential letter for the Pope — perhaps, indeed, the letter which was to bring the Cardinal's downfall. (Cf. Shakespeare's *Henry VIII.*)

the Council: the Privy Council, the King's appointed "cabinet".

a little common sense: It is significant that Wolsey, the man of power, echoes the expression just used by the Common Man in his role as Steward.

PAGE 11. *He's been to play in the muck again:* the first reference in the play to Henry's relationship with Anne Boleyn. Wolsey leaves no doubt of his own feelings in the matter.

a change of dynasty: The Royal House was established by Henry Tudor after his defeat of Richard III at the Battle of Bosworth (1485). His subsequent marriage united the Houses of York and Lancaster and, upon his death in 1509, his second and surviving son, Henry, became King.

Catherine's his wife: Catherine of Aragon (1485-1536), daughter of Ferdinand and Isabella of Spain. After her marriage to Henry was declared null and void, she became a literal exile from court. She turned to religious matters for her consolation and died in January of 1536.

a dispensation: in the Roman Catholic Church, an official exemption or release from the provisions of a specific Church Law. Since Catherine had married Prince Arthur (who had died in 1502) and since Church Law barred a man from marrying his brother's widow, a papal dispensation was necessary to permit her marriage to Henry. Henry and Catherine were married by proxy in 1503 and after many delays Pope Julius II issued his dispensation. In June of 1509, Catherine was wedded to Henry with full ceremony.

PAGE 12. *the Pope:* Clement VII was Pope from 1523 to 1534.

the Yorkist Wars: the Wars of the Roses (1455-85) between the Houses of York and Lancaster. Wolsey recalls them as a time of chaos when the succession was greatly in doubt.

he relights the candle: What symbolic value does More attach to this act?

PAGE 13. *Fisher:* John Fisher (1459-1535), the bishop of Rochester, an important figure in the religious world. As Queen Catherine's confessor, he opposed both the divorce and the doctrine of the royal supremacy. As Henry's only opponent among the bishops, he was eventually accused of high treason and put to death.

Suffolk: Charles Brandon (1485?-1545), first Duke of Suffolk, an opponent of Wolsey and loyal servant of Henry under whom he held various important positions.

PAGE 14. *Chapuys:* Eustace Chapuys, the Imperial ambassador. Serving the cause of Spain, he is portrayed throughout the play as a creature of intrigue.

PAGE 15. *Charles:* Charles V, King of Spain (1516-56) and Holy Roman Emperor (1519-56), was the nephew of Queen Catherine.

Dominus vobiscum ... spiritu tuo: "(May) the Lord be with you ... and with thy spirit." These expressions are found in various places of the Mass and used also as a common farewell.

PAGE 16. *The river looks very black tonight:* Note the double significance of this conversation.

Master Roper's here: William Roper (1496-1578). His book, *The Mirror of Virtue in Worldly Greatness or the Life of Sir Thomas More,* is one of the best biographies of his great father-in-law.

the Bar: the legal profession.

PAGE 17. *the City:* the commercial centre of London, an area today of roughly one square mile.

Doctor Luther: Martin Luther (1483-1546), German theologian and leader of the German Reformation.

Luther's an excommunicate: Luther had been excommunicated in 1520.

It's a shop: Roper means, of course, a place for making purchases. At this time, the sale of Indulgences was a common practice of the Church. It was partially against this that Luther rebelled.

The Inns of Court: where the law students lived, not to be confused with the King's Court.

Antichrist: the greatest opponent of Christ whose arrival would bring untold evil to the world until the Second Coming of Christ defeated him. See I *John* 2:18.

PAGE 18. *Oh, one more or less:* Here, as elsewhere, we see More's dismissal of bitter argument by a humorous touch.

PAGE 19. *the Tower:* the Tower of London, traditional place of confinement for prisoners of rank.

PAGE 20. *Whether we follow tradition:* Note that here the Common Man returns to his role at the beginning of the play — a character who is at once in the play and yet external to it. Note also that this speech neatly covers a gap of three to five years in the action.

Leicester: a city, county borough, and county town of Leicestershire. Wolsey died at the Abbey of St. Mary and was buried in the Lady Chapel.

charge of High Treason: Understandably, Wolsey had many enemies. They finally came against him. In 1529, he was indicted for praemunire and banished to the See of York. His communications with the Pope — in which he was supposed to urge Henry's excommunication — led to the charge of high treason.

by his writings: More's most famous works are his *History of Richard III* (upon which Shakespeare indirectly drew) and his *Utopia.*

Hampton Court: A large palace in Middlesex, it was built by Wolsey in 1515 and was yielded to Henry in 1526.

PAGE 21. *Deptford:* A borough of the county of London, some three miles southeast of the City, it had formerly a major dockyard.

the Great Harry: an anachronistic reference. Actually, the *Henri Grace à Dieu,* popularly known as the *Great Harry,* a ship "built loftie" and golden-sailed, had been launched much earlier. It was she who took Henry on his visit to King Francis in 1520.

PAGE 22. *Sir Thomas is a man:* What point is Cromwell making here?

PAGE 23. *Dominican:* a member of an order of mendicant friars, founded in 1215 by St. Dominic.

PAGE 24. *No man can serve two masters:* See *St. Matthew* 6:24.

PAGE 25. *a fanfare of trumpets; plainsong:* Note the playwright's clever blending of the two symbolic elements of State and Church. It is significant for More that "when the fanfare ceases the plainsong goes on quietly".

PAGE 26. *My Lord Chancellor:* This short incident with Norfolk is related in Roper's biography.

Vespers: the second last of the seven periods of each day, set aside by the Roman Catholic Church for prayer and worship.

PAGE 27. *Henry:* Now in the thirty-ninth year of his life and the twenty-first of his reign, Henry is here portrayed as a man of great vigour and many enthusiasms. He is younger and more volatile than the heavy, bellowing, many-wived monarch of the popular imagination.

PAGE 28. *There is no end to the making of books:* See *Ecclesiastes* 12:12.

PAGE 29. *Your Grace's Book:* In May, 1520, Henry had completed his *Assertio Septem Sacramentorum (Assertion of the Seven Sacraments)* as a reply to a work by Luther. The book argues for the authority of the Pope. In October of the same year, Pope Leo X conferred upon Henry the title, *Fidei Defensor* (Defender of the Faith) which, even after the quarrel with Rome, the King retained.

PAGE 30. *the Bishop of Rome:* one of the Pope's titles. Is Henry already thinking of the Pope as merely another bishop?

it was never merry in England: This remark is attributed to the Duke of Norfolk and was spoken in hostility to Wolsey.

Doggett's Bank: a fictional feature in the lower Thames.

Tilbury Roads: Tilbury is today an urban district of Essex, on the north bank of the Thames. It has extensive docking facilities and a protected, offshore area (Roads) where ships lie at anchor.

PAGE 31. *the Great Seal:* the emblem of the office of the Lord Chancellor.

Deuteronomy: See *Deuteronomy* 25:5.

PAGE 32. *the Holy See:* A See is the jurisdictional position or area of a bishop; the Holy See is the Apostolic Court of the Pope.

Son after son she's borne me: Queen Catherine had had four sons, none of whom had lived longer than a few weeks.

I have a daughter: Mary, born in 1516 and destined to become Queen (1553-58).

It is my bounden duty: Henry stresses that his desire for a divorce arises from his need and responsibility to establish the succession upon a son. It is an irony of history that the daughter, Elizabeth, born of his marriage to Anne Boleyn, would become one of England's greatest monarchs.

St. Peter: one of the Apostles of Jesus, considered the first Pope and Founder of the Christian Church.

Discovered: King Henry was a competent composer.

PAGE 33. *Princes of the Church:* the Bishops and Cardinals. Why would Henry scorn the use of the title?

with the Emperor's knife to his throat: Henry suggests that the Pope is being governed by more than doctrinal considerations. See "Historical Background" (page 105).

PAGE 34. *Woman, mind your house:* Notice that, with Alice's reply, there is a significant double meaning here.

PAGE 35. *Lady Anne:* Anne Boleyn (1507?-36) was born into a prominent family and spent part of her early life in France. Most historians date her relationship with Henry as early as 1523, but her name was not openly associated with him until the beginnings of his divorce. Her marriage to Henry was short and tragic. In September, 1533, she gave birth to a daughter, Elizabeth, the future Queen; in May, 1536, she was accused of adultery and beheaded.

a sacrament of the Church: More refers to the sacrament of marriage.

PAGE 36. *Joshua's trumpet:* Joshua, the successor to Moses, was commanded by God to bring about the destruction of Jericho. By blowing upon a trumpet he shattered the walls. See *Joshua 6.*

the money-changers in the temple: See *St. Matthew* 21:12 and *St. John* 2:13-16. Roper refers to the abuses against which he had previously protested.

Sophistication: Roper means that More's protests are a form of subtlety used to disguise his true feelings in the matter.

PAGE 39. *this is the golden calf:* a false god or idol. See *Exodus 32.*

Meloch: a god of the ancient Phoenicians and Ammonites which demanded horrible sacrifices.

PAGE 40. *Burgundy:* a table wine, either red or white, named after the former province of France.

PAGE 42. *Collector of Revenues for York:* York was and is, after Canterbury, the most important See in England.

High Constable: at this time, the highest rank in the officials of the Royal Household.

Sir Thomas Paget: presumably a fictitious name.

Secretary to the Council: Since Cromwell did not achieve this eminence until 1534, why at this point has the playwright given him this title?

May I say "friendship"?: Where and under what circumstances had Rich earlier discussed "friendship"?

PAGE 43. *the embankment:* the banks of the Thames.

ACT TWO

PAGE 48. *You wouldn't last six months in Spain:* The Inquisition was reorganized in Spain in 1478. Its purpose was to root out, often by torture and the stake, any traces of heresy.

That chain of office: the emblem of the Lord Chancellor.

the bishops in Convocation: Actually this Convocation acknowledged Henry as "Supreme Head" in February of 1531. In May, 1532, Convocation in its "Submission of the Clergy" yielded fully to Henry.

Canterbury: city of Kent and the ecclesiastical metropolis of England.

The Archbishop: William Warham, Archbishop of Canterbury from 1503 to 1532. He was succeeded by Thomas Cranmer.

the Act of Supremacy: This Act, which made Henry Supreme Head of all the Church in England (*Anglicana Ecclesia*), was not passed by Parliament until the fall of 1534. What dramatic purpose has the playwright fulfilled by this "adjustment" of history?

PAGE 49. *a faint radiance:* an aura of light which in the art of the times was usually depicted as surrounding the heads of the holy. A typical example of More's wit.

Socrates: the Greek philosopher (470?-399 B.C.), noted for his moderation and idealism.

Erasmus: Desiderius Erasmus (1466?-1536), Dutch humanist and theologian; a good friend of More's.

hemlock: a poison by means of which Socrates was put to death.

PAGE 50. *Dominus .. excellencis:* "The Lord be with you, my children .. And with you, Excellency."

PAGE 52. *Reformation:* More, like Erasmus, was an advocate of reform from within, not of open rebellion.

PAGE 53. *The Apostolic Succession:* the doctrine of the Roman Catholic Church that the authority conferred by Jesus upon St. Peter (See *St. Matthew* 16:17-19.) has come down in an unbroken line of the Bishops of Rome.

PAGE 54. *The King accepts your resignation:* More's resignation from the Chancellorship was accepted on May 16, 1532.

he will be your good lord: one of Henry's broken promises.

the Border: the troublesome boundary between England and Scotland.

the Old Alliance: the traditional, anti-English friendship between France and Scotland.

the Dago: a sneering reference to Chapuys.

sit by the fire: Nicholas Harpsfield (in his *Life of More*) quotes Lady More as asking, "Will you sit still by the fire, and make goslings [that is, simple designs] in the ashes with a stick as children do?"

PAGE 55. *Like David with a harp:* See I *Samuel* 16:14-23.

the marriage he'll then make: Henry secretly married Anne Boleyn on January 25, 1533, and on June 1 she became Queen.

PAGE 58. *Cato:* Cato the Elder (234-149 B.C.), Roman consul, famed for his incorruptibility.

PAGE 59. *Lincoln:* chief city of Lincolnshire, an eastern county lying between the Wash and the Humber River.

in April 1526: Note that this date establishes the time of the opening of the play.

PAGE 60. *Oh, this is a horse that won't run:* This particular attempt won't be successful.

PAGE 62. *I have a Royal Commission:* from the King of Spain, not from King Henry.

PAGE 63. *I have a personal letter for you:* This historical incident effectively points up More's political caution.

PAGE 64. *a huge bundle of bracken:* Harpsfield states that Sir Thomas "was enforced and compelled for lack of other fuel, every night before he went to bed, to cause a great bundle of fern to be brought into his own chamber and with the blaze whereof to warm himself, his wife and his children, and so without any other fires to go to their beds".

the money from the Bishops: Because they knew of his need, the clergy in Convocation offered More four thousand pounds. Officially it was offered him because of his many writings in defence of the Church.

PAGE 65. *There's a gentleman here from Hampton Court:* Roper's announcement advances the action to February of 1534, at which time More was brought before the Commissioners to answer certain "charges". Note the dramatic impact of having More meet, not the Commissioners, but Cromwell!

PAGE 66. *Wit's what's in question:* Notice the pun upon wit (keenness of intellect) and witty (humorous).

a pragmatist, the merest plumber: one who is concerned only for the practical results of an action.

That's a nice gown you have, Richard: What ironical point is More making here?

PAGE 67. *the Universities, the Bishops, and the Parliament of this realm:* By this time almost all the authorities — individuals and institutions — had yielded to the King's wishes.

Holy Maid of Kent: Elizabeth Barton (1506?-1534) was subject to religious mania, which included trances, periods of hysteria, and, she maintained, direct communications with the Virgin Mary. She inveighed against Henry's divorce and predicted his death. Through the work of Cromwell and Cranmer, she confessed her imposture and with her accomplices was executed. More said that her predictions were "such as any simple woman might speak out of her own wit".

PAGE 68. *the King published a book:* See the earlier note for page 29.

PAGE 69. *canon law:* Church Law.

These are terrors for children: When in February, 1534, a Bill of Attainder was introduced into the House of Lords, the names of More and Fisher were included. Before the Commissioners, More successfully answered the charges which Cromwell brings against him here, and added, "My Lords, these terrors be arguments for children, not for me."

PAGE 70. *They won't bring me a boat:* Note the symbolism of this point.

PAGE 71. *You're between the upper and nether millstones:* that is, in a position to be crushed.

We're supposed to be the arrogant ones: Norfolk refers, of course, to the nobility.

PAGE 72. *the Sermon on the Mount:* See *St. Matthew* 5-7.

Thomas Aquinas: St. Thomas Aquinas (1225?-74), one of the major philosophers of the Roman Catholic Church.

PAGE 73. *somewhere back along your pedigree —:* Notice that here More applies his earlier symbol of the water spaniel. As the dog is untrue to its own nature, so is Norfolk false to his own soul.

There's to be a new Act: the Act of Succession (March, 1534).

This Act preceded the Act of Supremacy (November, 1534), but the playwright has intentionally reversed the order because he wishes the discussion in the following scene to revolve around the historically earlier Act.

PAGE 74. *Iron grills now descend:* Here (the Tower), as elsewhere, a simple device serves to set the scene.

PAGE 75. *Bit nearer the knuckle:* colloquial English expression meaning "verging more on the unacceptable".

Cranmer: Thomas Cranmer (1489-1556) aided Henry in his divorce proceedings and became the Archbishop of Canterbury in 1533, at which time he officially granted the divorce. Ironically, it was he who later declared invalid Henry's marriage to Anne Boleyn. In the reign of Queen Mary, Cranmer was accused of high treason and put to death.

PAGE 79. *Some men think the Earth is round:* The theory of the Polish astronomer, Copernicus (1473-1543), had not yet been fully accepted.

I defy anyone to live in that cell for a year: More was committed to the Tower in mid-April, 1534.

PAGE 81. *the rack:* Cromwell's consideration of this instrument of torture sheds an interesting light upon his role as an opportunist.

PAGE 83. *If we lived in a State —:* Here More comments upon his own *Utopia*.

PAGE 84. *Well, has Eve run out of apples?:* More asks if his daughter has ceased her tempting.

PAGE 89. *the Hall of Westminster:* More was brought here on July 1, 1535.

My lords, I thank you: It is interesting to notice the playwright's ability in "tightening" this speech. Records indicate that More answered the charge by saying: "My Lords, I humbly thank you for your great good will. Howbeit, I make my petition unto Almighty God that it may please Him to maintain me in this my honest mind, to the last hour that I shall live. And concerning the matters you charge me withal, the articles are so prolix and long that I fear, what for my long imprisonment, what for my disease and present weakness, that neither my wit, nor memory, nor voice will serve to make sufficient answer."

PAGE 90. *Bishop Fisher was executed this morning:* Actually, Fisher was beheaded on June 22.

Death — comes for us all: In the Tower, More wrote, in his *Dialogue of Comfort against Tribulation:* "And therefore, but if he [a king] be a fool, he can never be without fear, that either on the morrow, or on the selfsame day, the grisly, cruel hangman, Death, which, from his first coming in, hath ever hovered aloof, and looked toward him, and ever lain in await on him, shall amid all his royalty, and all his main strength, neither kneel before him, nor make him any reverence, nor with any good manner desire him to come forth; but vigorously and fiercely gripe him by the very breast, and make all his bones rattle, and so by long and divers sore torments, strike him stark dead, and then cause his body to be cast into the ground in a foul pit, there to rot and be eaten with the wretched worms of the earth, sending yet his soul out farther unto a more fearful judgment, whereof at his temporal death his success is uncertain ... Knew you not that Christ must suffer passion, and by that way enter into his kingdom? Who can for very shame desire to enter into the kingdom of Christ with ease, when himself entered not into his own without pain?"

PAGE 95. *Southwell and Palmer:* Actually, both these men were present for the trial, and both denied Rich's testimony. What dramatic advantage is gained by having them absent?

The red dragon: the traditional emblem of Wales.

it profits a man nothing: See *St. Mark* 8:36.

PAGE 97. *Now we plainly see that you are malicious:* The Act of Treasons (passed in 1534) made it high treason, after February 1, 1535, by words or writing *maliciously* to deprive the King of his dignity, titles, or names of his royal estates. It is upon this point that Cromwell pounces.

PAGE 98. *My master had easel and gall:* Easel is vinegar. See *St. Matthew* 27:48.

QUESTIONS

(The questions which follow are organized according to the various scenes within the two acts.)

ACT ONE

SCENE I

(a) In what ways do the Common Man's words and actions prepare us for the subject matter and the nature of the play?

(b) What elements within the character of More are revealed through his introductory conversation with Rich?

(c) Discuss the symbolic value attached to the story of the falcon and the heron.

(d) Write a short sketch to show the difference in character between Alice and Margaret.

SCENE 2

(a) How do Wolsey and More differ in their approaches to the subject of the King's divorce?

(b) What proof is there that More, in matters of state, is a cautious man?

(c) What arguments does Wolsey advance in favour of Henry's having an heir?

(d) "The irony of the conversation between Wolsey and More is that Wolsey is the practical prelate while More is the idealistic layman." Discuss.

(e) What significance may be attached to the snuffing and the relighting of the candle?

SCENE 3

(a) What dramatic purposes are served by More's short conversations with Cromwell and Chapuys?

SCENE 4

(a) Discuss the aptness of the comment that Roper represents the intellectual ferment of the times.

(b) What evidence have we of More's affection for his daughter?

SCENE 5

(a) Why does the playwright have the Common Man read a passage of historical writing?

(b) What proof may we find to show that Cromwell is a crafty and clever man?

(c) Show that in this scene the amateur (the Common Man) has outwitted the professionals.

SCENE 6

(a) From his interview with the King show that More is a man of subtle humour.

(b) By means of four specific illustrations, support the comment that Henry possesses a volatile nature.

(c) What evidence have we of Henry's dissatisfaction with Rome?

(d) What proof does Henry offer as justification for his proposed course of action?

(e) Trace the development of the King's thought from the introduction of the subject of divorce to his conclusion, "I have no Queen!"

(f) How do Henry and More differ in their natures?

(g) "Henry's serious comments to More are a combination of flattery and subtle threat." Discuss.

(h) What modification do we now find in Roper's "views"?

(i) For what reason does Roper accuse More of "sophistication"?

(j) What arguments does More use in support of "Man's law"?

(k) What evidence have we in this scene that More is not as unconcerned as he perhaps appears?

SCENE 7

(a) What proof is there in these last two scenes of Act One for the judgment of history that Rich was a "time-server"?

(b) Outline briefly Cromwell's theory of "convenience".

(c) What elements within the character of Cromwell suggest that he will play a significant role in Act Two?

ACT TWO

SCENE 1

(a) From the Common Man's introduction and from the short conversation between Roper and More, what necessary information does the audience learn?

(b) Discuss the attitude of More to the probing of Chapuys and to the news which Norfolk brings.

(c) How do the members of More's family react to his resignation?

(d) What evidence have we in this scene of More's political wisdom?

SCENE 2

(a) From this scene, what would appear to be the forthcoming and individual roles of Norfolk, Rich, and Cromwell?

SCENE 3

(a) What characteristics of More are revealed by his refusal to accept (i) Charles's letter, (ii) the money from the clergy?

SCENE 4

(a) What are the "charges" which Cromwell brings against More and how does the latter successfully counter them?

(b) In what position does More find himself at the end of this conversation?

SCENE 5

(a) Outline fully the process whereby More "destroys" his friendship with Norfolk.

(b) Explain in detail why More refuses to submit to Henry.

(c) State concisely the course of action which he proposes to Margaret and Roper.

SCENE 6

(a) What is More's defence before the Seventh Commission?

SCENE 7

(a) In what ways does Margaret "tempt" her father?

(b) "Alice shows that she is caught between her love for her husband and her annoyance at his stubbornness." Discuss.

SCENE 8

(a) Explain Cromwell's reply to More's defence of "silence".

(b) Summarize the "evidence" of Rich.

(c) "More's conduct throughout the trial is one of placid assurance." Discuss.

SCENE 9

(a) What further evidence have we in this last scene that More accepts his fate with sublime dignity?

GENERAL QUESTIONS

1. For each of the following passages, name the speaker, give the context, and briefly explain the significance of the speech:

(a) We must pray that when your head's finished turning your face is to the front again.

(b) You know it amazes me that you, who were once so effective *in* the world, and are now *so* much retired from it, should be opposing yourself to the whole movement of the times.

(c) The law is a causeway upon which so long as he keeps to it a citizen may walk safely.

(d) If you could come with me, you are the man I should soonest raise — yes, with my own hand.

(e) Oh, you'd walk on the bottom of the sea and think yourself a crab if he suggested it.

(f) I believe, when statesmen forsake their own private consciences for the sake of their public duties — they lead their country by a short route to chaos.

2. On a number of occasions Sir Thomas More is tempted to a course of action repugnant to his nature. State briefly four such occasions and discuss his reaction to each of them.

3. At several points throughout the play, the playwright heightens our interest by a hint of some future action. Pick out four examples of this foreshadowing and outline briefly the incidents which fulfil each of them.

4. In his Preface, Mr. Bolt states, "Thomas More, as I wrote about him, became for me a man with an adamantine sense of his own self." Find and comment upon several specific incidents in which More points up his consciousness of "the self".

5. Discuss with suitable illustrations three means which enable the development of the plot to flow smoothly from scene to scene.

6. Define symbolism. Find five examples of this device and show clearly the appropriateness of each.

7. On the scaffold More is reported to have said that he was "the King's good servant, but God's first". By means of at least three references to *A Man for All Seasons*, prove the validity of this final comment.

8. Robert Bolt states that the part of the Common Man employs "the most notorious of the alienation devices". (a) Explain what the playwright means by this expression. (b) Show by three illustrations the means which he has used to overcome the Common Man's "alienation".

9. By reference to the quotation from Robert Whittinton (see Frontispiece), explain the appropriateness of the title of this play.

10. In a concise paragraph for each, define the roles of the following characters: Rich, Margaret, Chapuys, Alice, and the woman from Lincoln.

11. Compare and contrast Norfolk and Cromwell as men who are willing to follow "the whole movement of the times".

12. "Throughout the play, More displays a subtle, ironic wit." Find at least four occasions which support the aptness of this judgment.

13. Mr. Bolt describes Roper as possessing "an all consuming rectitude which is his cross, his solace, and his hobby". By means of references to different parts of the play, prove the truth of this description.

14. A tragic hero is briefly defined as a noble human being possessed of a flaw in his character. State why you agree or disagree with the suitability of applying this definition to Sir Thomas More.

15. For Shakespeare's *King Lear* and Bolt's *A Man for All Seasons*, briefly compare and contrast the value and use of each of the following.
(a) humour as a means to emphasize the serious action;
(b) the introduction of minor characters as a comment upon major figures;
(c) a scene of tension to point up the play's essential conflict;
(d) the swift flow of action from scene to scene.

16. Both Sir Thomas More and King Lear are men of great individuality. Discuss the extent to which each, because of this individuality, rises or falls in our estimation.

17. In both *King Lear* and *A Man for All Seasons*, the female characters have considerable influence over the course of the action. Comment upon the aptness of this remark. You should be able to argue both *for* and *against* the comment.

QUESTIONS ON THE FILM OF

*A Man for All Seasons**

A film version of *A Man for All Seasons* was released in 1966 and won six Oscars, including Best Picture and Best Actor (Paul Scofield). Robert Bolt himself wrote the screenplay and won the Best Screenplay Oscar for his work. Some of the following questions, which form a film study of *A Man for All Seasons*, indicate minor differences between the stage play and the film version and offer an interesting comparison of the two mediums.

1. The film begins with an action, the stage play with a speech by the Common Man.

    (a) Sum up in a brief statement your opinion of the merits of each technique. Which do you prefer? Why?

    (b) Within the full concept of the film, discuss the significance of each of the following features which precede the list of credits:

        (i) the initial shot of the King's Beasts
        (ii) the close-up of Wolsey's chain of office
        (iii) Wolsey's silent action in the sealing and giving of the letter
        (iv) the presence of the people outside the Chancellor's office
        (v) the open door
        (vi) the dawn and the waterfowl
        (vii) the flowing Thames
        (viii) the music

° *A 16 mm. version of the film "A Man for All Seasons" is available through Columbia Pictures of Canada Limited, 72 Carlton Street, Toronto, Ontario (Attention: 16 mm. Department).*

PAUL SCOFIELD AS SIR THOMAS MORE

2. What initial impressions are created by the people assem-
bled at Sir Thomas More's house? Consider the nature and
position of Matthew, the relationship between More and
his wife and daughter, the presence of Norfolk, and the
ambiguous status of Rich.

3. "There's no art/To find the mind's construction in the face," says Shakespeare's King Duncan, not perhaps the most acute judge of character.

   (a) Write a brief sketch of what you find portrayed in the faces of the following:
      (i) Wolsey *loyal to his work*
      (ii) Rich *worm*
      (iii) Matthew
      (iv) More *A man for all Seasons*

   (b) What speeches or actions within the stage play support your analyses of these men?

4. (a) What features in the scene between More and Wolsey intensify the differences of personality between the two?

   (b) What is the dramatic value of having Cromwell outside the door?

   (c) Why has the film added the two petitioners who greet More as he leaves?

   (d) What significance do More's attempt to throw away the silver cup and his later offer of it to Rich have at this point in the story's development?

5. Neither the scene of Wolsey's death nor that of More's installation as Chancellor occurs in the play. Why have these been added to the film? What photographic techniques increase the effectiveness of these two short scenes?

6. (a) What evidence does the film present that, despite what one might call the *moral* superiority of Sir Thomas More, King Henry's is the social and constitutional superiority?

   (b) Discuss the roles played in this episode of Henry's visit to Chelsea by:
      (i) the nobles who accompany Henry
      (ii) the commoners who watch him
      (iii) Rich and Cromwell

   (c) In what ways do sound, colour, and movement contribute to the effectiveness of this episode?

7. Examine closely the stage and film scenes of the tavern meeting between Rich and Cromwell.

    (a) What changes in dialogue and action has the playwright made?

    (b) In what ways does the film scene expand upon the stage scene?

    (c) State which scene you prefer and justify your choice.

8. Outline the evidence which the film reveals of the increasing poverty of the Mores. Which aspect of this increasing poverty did you find most effectively presented?

9. The "King's Business" — his divorce and remarriage — is quickly handled by a series of brief and clever scenes.

    (a) Discuss the purpose of the scene with the bishops.

    (b) What advantage is there in the addition of a *silent* Anne Boleyn to the cast?

    (c) What dramatic purposes are served by the song and by King Henry's momentary identification of a wedding guest as Sir Thomas?

    (d) Why are we given a very brief tour of certain English churches? How might the same effect be achieved in a stage presentation?

10. From the trial scene, pick out and discuss the effectiveness of *three* film techniques which a stage direction might find awkward if indeed not impossible to achieve.

11. "The 'successful' career of Richard Rich is cleverly reflected in his costume changes throughout the film." Discuss.

12. (a) From the standpoint of dramatic technique and for the value of clarifying the theme of this work, what merit is there in the final, anonymous comment in the film?

    (b) How else might the film have ended? Why? Draw from your imagination at least three other possibilities and justify the virtues of each.

THE TRIAL SCENE

13. The roles of the Spanish Ambassador and of the Common Man as narrator were both removed from the film.

    (a) How do you account for these changes?

    (b) Explain why you agree or disagree with them.

    (c) If they were necessary to the stage play, how has the film made good their loss?

14. The action of *A Man for All Seasons* covers a number of years.

    (a) Write a brief note setting forth the limits of that time.

(b) Explain how the playwright has dealt with the passing of time in his stage work.

(c) Explain and illustrate with at least four references the contrasting technique of the film.

(d) State which technique you prefer and justify your choice.

15. Discuss the use made of climate, the world of nature, the seasons, and the time of day as reflections upon the action and theme of the drama. How and why does the emphasis in the film differ from that in the stage play?

16. By his position in the auditorium, the playgoer is fixed to a physical point of view; the filmgoer, even while remaining in his seat, is permitted, through the eyes of the camera, to watch the action from a number of vantage points. Using any major scene from *A Man for All Seasons*, defend the merits of both stage and film technique.

17. Choose a scene of vigorous action and account for its effectiveness within the framework of the story. Then choose a scene of quiet thoughtfulness and explain its value. Why are both scenes necessary to the film?

18. In the Preface to this book (pages vii to xix), Robert Bolt discusses his very considerable use of metaphor, of imagery, of symbolism. Pick out any *five* recurring symbols and discuss their effectiveness within the context of the shifting times and moods of the action.

19. Discuss the *relative* importance of plot (and theme), setting, and characterization to the success of this film. Point out where you feel the director has let his emphasis lie and explain why you agree or disagree with him.

20. Suppose that you were asked to add *one* scene to this film.

(a) Outline the content of that scene.

(b) Write the few pages of dialogue that the scene would require.

(c) Explain any special photographic techniques which you might wish to use.

THE EXECUTION

Jonathan Playfair